TEEN ANGELS

TO MEL HEATH (1972–2

Educational Publishers LLP trading as BBC Active
Edinburgh Gate
Harlow
Essex CM20 2JE
England

First published 2006

ISBN 0 563 52008 6

Commissioning Editor: Emma Shackleton
Project Editor: Patricia Burgess
Designer: Annette Peppis
Cover image design: The Station
Indexer: Margaret Cornell
Senior Production Controller: Man Fai Lau

Set in Frutiger and Scala
Printed in Italy by Rotolito Lombarda

The Publisher's policy is to use paper manufactured from sustainable forests.

TEEN ANGELS

Dr Stephen Briers &
Sacha Baveystock

BBC ACTIVE

Contents

1 Help, I've got a   6
  teenager!

2 Get ready for change 16

3 Shut up!   32

4 Whose life is it   52
  anyway?

5 Boundaries and the   68
  bottom line

6 Under pressure   92

7 Teen building   118

8 Family matters   132

And finally...   145
Further information   147
Acknowledgements   153
Index   155

chapter one

Help, I've got a teenager!

WHEN WE STARTED RESEARCHING THE BBC3 SERIES *TEEN ANGELS* OUR TEAM members would often visit families at home. There on the wall or table would be photos of happy, smiling families, often bearing little resemblance to the unhappy teenager and grim-faced parents being interviewed.

'We used to get along fine,' the parents would cry. 'But now he [or she] has *changed*!' Meanwhile, the teen would shrug: 'They're fussing too much. They're always on my back. It's not my problem...'

It's a situation you may recognize. However well prepared you think you are, it's still a shock to find your happy, easygoing child has been replaced overnight by someone else: most likely a moody, self-obsessed and argumentative creature, who raids the fridge, uses you as a taxi service and seems to care more about what his friends think than how his behaviour is affecting you. You ask yourself: 'Where did it all go wrong?'

But from your teenager's point of view it seems like nothing *you* do is right. Every effort to be encouraging and supportive is brushed aside, and you feel like you're blamed for everything that's wrong with his life. Tempers keep flaring and the whole family is feeling the strain.

It can be hard not to take it personally, but if any of that sounds familiar, take comfort from the fact that there are many others like you. As the makers of the popular BBC3 parenting series *Little Angels*, which concentrated on younger children, we got frequent calls from the parents of teenagers who were struggling to cope with the challenges of adolescence. Many of them had tried reading books, asking advice from health professionals, teachers or other parents, but they just didn't know which way to turn. And so *Teen Angels* was born.

How to get your very own Teen Angel

Like the families we've met during the making of two series of *Teen Angels*, if you're raising teens, you've undoubtedly entered one of the most challenging phases in your life as a parent. But there are ways of navigating these stormy waters, and by using examples from these families, we hope to show you how. The aim of this book is to help you understand more fully the conflict in your life and learn ways of defining the nature of each problem. Most importantly with teenagers, our aim is to show you which problems you can do something about, and where to draw the line with those that you can't.

In *Little Angels*, the message we gave to parents was a simple one: look at your own behaviour and see how it is affecting that of your child. With teenagers, the picture is more complex, but the essence of that advice remains the same. For the families who took part in *Teen Angels* this was an opportunity for the parents to stand back, take a look at what was happening and think about new ways of moving forward.

Your own behaviour tape

Before you can get to grips with the problems you are facing, you must first become more aware of what is really going on. That's why we asked every family who took part in *Teen Angels* to agree to an initial fortnight of potentially revealing, no-holds-barred filming in their homes. With their permission, fixed cameras with motion sensors were mounted in the main living spaces to film the family behaving in their usual way. In addition, teens went out with a film crew, or were loaned small cameras to take out with them to record aspects of their own lives that their parents might not necessarily see. This material was edited together to make a 'behaviour tape' that series experts Tanya Byron, Stephen Briers and Laverne Antrobus would view and then show to the family.

For the families, seeing themselves interacting on tape always had a powerful effect. Although they were aware that they had been filmed, they were suddenly able to see the conflict they were experiencing from a new (and not always flattering) perspective. The teens were often fascinated and sometimes ashamed to see how difficult they were being. For the parents it could be a moment of realizing how they came across too, and how their own patterns of behaviour were not always helping the situation.

Playing this material back to a family could be potentially explosive. When 13-year-old James Ellis saw how his mother searched his school bag every day, he was outraged. But it created an opportunity for his mother to reveal how little she trusted him. Similarly, Robert Kingdon's mother, Julie Hunt, was devastated when she saw footage of him drinking at the recreation ground, but it enabled Robert to admit that he preferred the recreation ground to staying at home, and forced his parents to begin confronting some of the reasons why.

While we don't recommend that you start following your teenager around with a camera, it will help to start considering how his behaviour might appear if viewed objectively through a camera lens. It's also worth imagining that the camera is watching you too. How would the average exchange with your teen appear on screen? By creating your own imaginary behaviour tape you'll be one step closer to identifying the root of your problem.

Keeping a diary

Since you can't really mount cameras in your home, we recommend that you start to keep a very simple, and private, diary that 'observes' for you. It will help you to recognize patterns of behaviour and flashpoints for your problems. It could also help you think about how you are responding to your teenage child when she is behaving in ways you don't like. Having a clear description of what is happening may also provide a useful launch pad for discussion with your teenager, who might well see the situation very differently.

We will give you more detail about how to use your diary in the next chapter. For the time being, however, we suggest you start by keeping a record of every occasion when you and your teen fall out. Note down a brief description of the situation in which the behaviour took place, what was going on at the time and any events that led up to the behaviour in question. Describe briefly what happened and how both you and your teen reacted. Also consider the final outcome: what happened as a result?

If you can bear to, it's worth keeping your diary for at least two weeks before you start to make any changes. It's important to understand the true nature of your problems before you start trying to change things. Only when you've got a full and clear picture can you start to act effectively.

Problem teenager or teenage problem?

While we're using the word 'problem' a lot, it's worth remembering that much of what you're experiencing is likely to be normal. To start to understand that, you need to think about how things are from your teenager's point of view. While his teenage years may be turning your hair grey, it is important to remember that underneath that dismissive or defiant exterior your adolescent child is under pressure too. Poised between childhood and adulthood, an adolescent has to cope with a whole range of developmental changes.

Between the ages of ten and 18 your child's body undergoes a dramatic revolution. A cocktail of hormones feeds the growth of secondary sexual characteristics, such as facial hair in boys and breasts in girls. Surges in the hormones testosterone and oestrogen will provide novel physical experiences – unexpected ejaculations for boys, periods for girls, and an awakening of sexual drives and tensions for both sexes.

All this is accompanied by a rapid acceleration of growth in every part of the body. Physical proportions alter dramatically, as fat/muscle ratios are rebalanced. The weight of the average human heart actually doubles during this period. Your teenager may swiftly find herself in a much larger, reshaped body that feels very alien.

If you can cast your mind back to your own teenage years, you may remember how awkward these physical changes made you feel. Looking, sounding and feeling so different within such a short space of time can be a very disconcerting experience, often accompanied by excruciating clumsiness and self-consciousness.

You may remember the moods that accompany these changes too. Raised testosterone levels in your boy might make him uncharacteristically aggressive, while your daughter's fluctuating hormone levels as her periods gradually become established could make her unusually moody or over-sensitive. Sixteen-year-old Anni Ellis would fly off the handle at the slightest remark from her mother. This is quite typical behaviour for a teenage girl whose hormones are going through upheaval.

Puberty also takes place at different rates and ages among boys and girls. At 12 or 13 some girls are virtually physically mature, while others may still be awaiting their growth spurt. Among boys there can be a five-year variation in the age at which they reach puberty. Comparing himself with peers who may be developing more or less rapidly can undermine your child's self-confidence or alter his relationship with both peers and siblings. Sexual maturity also presents your child with all sorts of new possibilities when she doesn't yet have the experience to handle them confidently.

So it's not surprising that teenagers are preoccupied with their physical appearance, or that there's so much adolescent angst about their bodies. For the Parkinson sisters, Lucie and Elane, looking good and feeling good were closely connected, and this is common. For many teenagers there's a close link between their self-esteem and how comfortable they feel with their body image.

If you imagine how teenagers are getting used to all these physical changes at the same time as having to deal with the pressures of exams, new relationships and increasing involvement with their peers, it's no wonder that they can sometimes feel highly stressed.

Who am I?

David and Julie Hunt were concerned that 15-year-old Robert was too involved with a gang of friends, who seemed to be drawing him away from the family and turning him into someone they found hard to recognize. It was difficult for them to understand that this was Robert's way of trying to establish a new and independent identity, whatever the risks involved.

Establishing an independent personal identity is one of the major tasks facing an adolescent, and it's not as easy as it may sound. Although children know from infancy that they are physically separate beings, they use relationships with family members as the main way of defining themselves while they are growing up. Until he hits his teenage years, a child depends on his family to hold up the mirror and reflect back to him who he is.

As your child reaches adolescence, he turns to a whole range of additional influences, including friends, role models, popular culture and new experiences outside the home. It's during this time that the difficult process of self-definition starts in earnest, and that might mean rejecting some of those familiar images previously supplied by the family. Teens may start looking to other relationships or groups to give them new and preferred visions of themselves, and may go through many different experimental stages.

Recklessness and experimentation are common features in adolescents trying to develop a new sense of self. For Robert this meant his first brushes with the law, as he tried to keep up with the gang's bravado. For Suraj De this meant some heavy partying as a means of breaking away from his mother's focus on educational achievement. However hard it seems, such behaviour is usually normal, and more often than not a passing phase. What's vitally important is how you react to it.

Breaking away

Adolescence is also the time when, psychologically, your child is preparing to leave home and make her own way in the world. Whatever their extravagant claims, this is secretly a terrifying prospect for many teens, who fear underneath that they lack the necessary experience and resources.

But this won't stop your teenager from thinking she can act like an adult. The desire for more independence drives many teenagers to demand excessive levels of freedom while they're still unprepared to take on any more responsibility. Like 16-year-old Jennie Manson, they may deliberately alienate their parents through angry, provocative or rejecting behaviour.

But this can quickly change too. It's not unusual for adolescents to ricochet between responsibility and neediness. While insisting that she knows it all, your teenager's cocky self-reliance can easily collapse, and you can suddenly be presented with a vulnerable, dependent child who desperately needs your reassurance and comfort. If keeping track of her rapidly changing needs can be confusing for you, just think what it must be like for her.

Younger teens especially may need to preserve a sense of connection with their parents. It is important not to assume that your child wants more independence when what he may need from you is more time and attention. At 13, James Ellis was being encouraged to entertain himself, but actually craved more involvement with his parents, particularly going golfing with his father. Getting this balance right can be tricky, and needs careful negotiating with your teenager. The fact remains that most teens benefit from continuing to spend time with their parents.

Fears about inadequacy or powerlessness can also affect teenage behaviour in other ways. They may seek to dominate others, or create conflicts in which they can assert themselves and try out what it feels like to sit in the driver's seat. Like Lucie Parkinson, who wanted to stay out late on a school night, many teenagers will relentlessly push at boundaries almost as a matter of course. Don't be fooled into thinking that this behaviour is just about trying to get their own way. When teens behave like this they are also testing you to see whether you can show the consistency and strength they secretly want for themselves.

'I just want to live for today,' insisted Suraj De. In truth, many teens have all sorts of fears about the future, which they may try to avoid by doggedly pursuing the 'rush' provided by sex, shopping, drugs or other sources of instant gratification. More anxious teenagers may start withdrawing their commitment to the activities that might connect them to the world of adult responsibilities, such as doing their school work. Helping them negotiate these pitfalls – and persuading them to listen to you – may take much patience and ingenuity.

Your job as a parent

Keeping your teen on track through these challenging years might seem like a daunting and, at times, thankless task. It's important to remember that adolescence causes some upheaval within most families, and it's only natural that it might make you question your ability as a parent. But despite your teenager's best efforts to push you away, your child probably needs you more than ever during this difficult and confusing time. Most importantly, how you handle these critical teenage years is also likely to influence your future relationship with your child once she is a fully grown adult.

Your job is to help your teenager experiment with increasing independence while providing the safety net at home. Although peer groups do become enormously influential on issues such as fashion and social behaviour, research suggests that parents remain the adolescent's main point of reference in a number of key areas, such as educational choices, careers and morality.

Research has also shown that children with high levels of self-esteem tend to be much less likely to be affected by peer pressure, misuse alcohol or be drawn into delinquent behaviour during adolescence. Given how precarious a teenager's self-worth can be, there is a vital role for parents to play in helping him to feel good about himself.

In the following chapters we will introduce you to some of the techniques that helped the families in the *Teen Angels* series cope with the challenges they were facing with their own teenagers. These parents were often able to regain control in situations that were at times pushing them to their limits. Ultimately, you know your child best; our aim is to provide you with some useful tools that you can adapt to your particular situation and the needs of your own teenager.

POINTS TO REMEMBER
○ To get the best out of your teen try to remember the developmental challenges your child is facing.
○ Learning how to read some of your teenager's more difficult behaviour may help you pick your battles more effectively.
○ You can learn and develop strategies to help your teen get what she wants in less destructive ways.
○ Your job as a parent is to retain a supportive environment and keep channels of communication going – no matter how tricky your teen's behaviour.
○ As with younger children, your own relationship with your teen may well provide the best starting point for understanding what is going wrong.
○ Try not to let your teen push you away. Whatever she may say or do, she probably needs you now more than ever.

chapter two

Get ready for change

'THEY WON'T TAKE A BLIND BIT OF NOTICE OF ME – THEY JUST WILL NOT DO ANY-thing I ask them to do,' sighed Glynis Gibson of her 15-year-old twin sons Luke and Jonny. Like many of the parents who contacted *Teen Angels*, Glynis felt she'd lost control. 'The boys don't live with me, I live with the boys, because they rule the roost in this house. They have no respect for it whatsoever.'

If you've been going through a rough time with your teenager, you may share this sense of deep frustration. You want your teen's behaviour to change, but at the same time you're probably feeling quite defeated and have no idea how to bring this change about.

When your child's behaviour is driving you up the wall it is only natural to focus upon him as the source of the problem. After all, you think, if it weren't for him, everything would be fine. For Glynis and her husband Rob, trouble with their twin sons had been steadily mount-ing. They had been excluded from mainstream school and now ran amok, while Glynis worked night shifts and Rob was away lorry-driving. Friends of the boys dropped in and out of the house, and they played loud techno music until late into the night. Most of Glynis's attempts to get them to do anything, including getting up in the morning, were greeted with a resounding 'F*** off'.

'Where do you go from here?' asked Rob in desperation. 'If you've tried everything, what do you do?' Certainly it was time for Luke and Jonny to start taking responsibility for their own actions; but Glynis and

Rob's negative belief that they could not do anything with their sons was in fact making things worse. By seeing the boys as the crux of the problem, Glynis and Rob were missing the one dimension of the situation where they did have full control – namely their *own* behaviour.

Glynis needed help to see that the way she reacted to the twins' behaviour – pleading with them to get up, for example, while not setting any consequences for the way they swore at her – was simply perpetuating the cycle of foul behaviour. Without any culture of respect in the house, it was impossible for the parents to get the teenagers to do what they asked. And as the parents continued to fund the boys' lifestyle no matter how they behaved, there was no incentive for the boys to change.

If you're reading this and thinking, 'So now it's all my fault, is it?', you may be missing the message. What's important to understand is that behaviour – especially objectionable behaviour – rarely occurs in a vacuum. There's always a reason for it, and the way in which you respond to it can be an important part of the pay-off that makes the behaviour worth continuing. By playing the victim while her sons swore at her, and continuing to fund their unruly lifestyle, Glynis was in fact enabling her twins to go on behaving badly – even though she hated it.

So if you're feeling that it's impossible to change the situation, it's time to take a step back and look at the whole picture. If you can develop a better understanding of the forces that are driving your teen's bad behaviour, when and where it happens, and the role you are playing in it, you will be taking the first step towards breaking the stalemate between you. Although you cannot force your son or daughter to change, you can change the way you react to them, which could transform the entire situation.

Play detective: keep a diary

Before you can decide what changes you might be able to make, you need to understand better what might be triggering and driving your teenager's difficult behaviour. Keeping a diary can help provide clues.

Below is the diary that Sue Watts might have kept detailing some of the very frustrating exchanges she had with her 16-year-old son Suraj. Sue had become extremely worried by Suraj's behaviour and was terrified that he was jeopardizing his future by messing up at college. Suraj in turn was determined to have a good time. The more Sue nagged him, the more entrenched he became. 'I'm having fun and that's what matters to me,' he insisted.

SAMPLE BEHAVIOUR DIARY

Situation – time and place	What I did	What he did	Outcome – what was the result?
Morning – worried that Suraj is late for college.	Made his breakfast, woke him up, told him I was worried he'd be late.	Told me he didn't have to go in until 11. Very rude. Told me he'd dropped English, and if I didn't believe him, I could ring the college. Walked out.	I felt upset, worried about his college work.
Friday night – Suraj going out drinking with friends.	Made him a sandwich to eat as he's going out drinking. Reminded him to eat it in front of his friends.	He pulled a face and swore at me in front of friends when I asked him to bring sandwich downstairs if he wasn't going to eat it.	I was humiliated in front of his friends and the sandwich wasn't eaten. Worried about him.
Evening – there is a college meeting tomorrow to discuss the final warning that Suraj has got. I want to discuss the meeting with him.	Tried to talk to him, following him from kitchen to bedroom. Sat on his bed and tried to get his attention.	He wouldn't talk to me, walked away, put on headphones and started swearing at me, saying he wasn't listening. He refused to talk.	I was completely frustrated by his behaviour and worried about his future at college.

On closer examination, what Sue's diary reveals is that nearly every row with her son was triggered by her anxiety about the situation – yet none of these conversations helped soothe her fears. While her concerns about what was happening to Suraj were all valid ones, these constant heated exchanges suggest that she needed to find another way of raising these issues with her son. Sue's worrying was making Suraj feel that she treated him like a child, which in turn was triggering childish responses from him. Sue was insistent that while he behaved so badly, she felt she had to treat him like a child, but she was unable to see that until Suraj began to take responsibility for his own actions, nothing would change.

By analysing these rows, Sue could begin to work out what the trigger was for their repeated arguments. There are many other scenarios that, when analysed, may reveal consistent patterns or situations that are clearly prompting your teen's more difficult behaviour.

Lucie and Elane Parkinson were so insecure that they competed constantly with each other for their mum Helen Ryan's attention. As fashion-conscious teens, they always wanted to go shopping – but shopping trips were a nightmare, with each daughter insisting that their mother was buying the other daughter more things. These trips were guaranteed to make the girls start acting like needy toddlers, complete with foot stamping, whining and sometimes tears, while Helen constantly felt the need to defend herself against accusations of favouritism. 'You cannot give them everything that they want because even if you did, or attempted to, it wouldn't stop – they'd still want more,' she complained.

But Helen had to be shown that she was actually unwittingly keeping this behaviour going by giving in to the girls' demands. Meanwhile, she was putting herself under increasing emotional and financial strain in her efforts to provide, making the situation even more tense.

Identifying triggers

If by now you've started filling in your diary and collecting some examples of your own teen's more challenging behaviour, your detective work can begin. The most important thing for you to spot is the trigger – what it was that made the situation go the way it did.

Take the time to sit down and review your diary. See whether you can spot some of the relevant factors, paying particular attention to anything you might be doing that could be provoking the behaviour you don't want. Look at your diary and ask yourself the following questions:

○ What was going on at the time the behaviour occurred? Are there particular situations in which the behaviour seems to occur more frequently?

○ If the behaviour takes place in a range of situations, are there any common links between them?

○ Is there anything you are doing that seems to produce the behaviour you don't like or make it worse? If you are having problems thinking about this and are feeling robust enough, try asking your teen. Most teenagers will be more than happy to point out what aspects of your actions and attitudes push their buttons. They will also be secretly pleased that you are prepared to shoulder some responsibility for the problem, and take their point of view seriously.

○ If you wanted to generate more rather than less of the behaviour in question, what could you do?

○ Are there times or situations when your teen does not produce the unwanted behaviour? Can you identify elements that are missing or different from the times in which she does?

○ What were you feeling and thinking just before your teen's undesirable behaviour occurred? Were you tired, stressed or in a hurry? How were those feelings and thoughts affecting your own actions and behaviour?

What's the pay-off?

Once you've started identifying some of the things that might be triggering your teenager's bad behaviour, you can start to think more about the function of that behaviour – in other words, what is your teen getting out of it? When trying to spot the *triggers*, you should pay attention to what happens before the unwanted behaviour takes place. However, to understand the *function* of your teen's behaviour, you need to look at what happens afterwards. Check through your diary again and ask yourself the following questions:

○ What happened afterwards? How did you respond?

○ How did your son or daughter's actions leave you feeling?

○ Did your teenager benefit in any way from what took place during the aftermath?

All these questions can provide you with important information about what your son or daughter is really trying to achieve by acting up.

It's important not to take your teenager's behaviour at face value, but rather to see it as a means to an end – even if the behaviour is objectionable or self-defeating. Sometimes the rewards for the behaviour may not be immediately obvious, but one thing is certain: if your child is continuing to act in a certain way, he is doing so because, at some level, it is working for him. So finding out what motivates your teen means that you may be able to help him find less destructive ways of getting his needs met.

With younger children there are often two clear motives for difficult behaviour: the need for attention, and the desire for control. With teenagers these two motives may still apply, but a range of other factors can also play a part. As teens are more sophisticated, the reasons underlying their behaviour may be more complex, and the way in which they seek to achieve their goals less obvious. Below are some examples of the motives that may be driving your teenager's behaviour and the way in which a parent's response can help either to extinguish or fuel the problem.

Look at me!

Sixteen-year-old Jennie Manson had developed a reputation for being disruptive, rude and rebellious. She wouldn't do what she was told, and could be relied upon to create drama and chaos around her wherever she went. At home Jennie's relationship with her stepdad Ian had reached breaking point, with constant rows about rules and timekeeping. Jennie knew full well that she could press Ian's buttons by challenging his rigid values. These had been formed during Ian's lifelong military career, which placed a high value on respecting rules and authority.

Jennie was looking for attention, and, like a little child who prefers being told off to being ignored, she was quite prepared for that attention to be negative. She made sure her stepfather fed her own need for negative attention by provoking terrible rows. Only later, when the arguments had died down, was Jennie able to admit how much attention the rows had given her. 'I think that's why I started being naughty in the first place,' she confessed.

Attention is a universal human need, and teenagers are no different in wanting it too. Whether they're aware of it or not, all teenagers face the prospect of having to move forward into a phase of life in which they will no longer be able to rely on their parents to meet all their emotional needs. As their awareness expands, teens have to face the realization that the world is a very big place, and that whatever they may have thought when they were younger, it no longer revolves around them.

All these realities can induce intense anxiety. Many teenagers respond by going through a period of being very self-centred, appearing unable to think about the needs of anyone around them. They may also deal with the dawning sense of their own insignificance by adopting behaviour that will be guaranteed to put them back in the spotlight – even if that means playing the villain or clown rather than the hero or heroine.

Jennie's shouting, swearing and coming in late for meals was guaranteed to keep her centre stage in the busy life of her family. But deep down she also felt hurt by Ian's lack of praise, and the sense that she was failing to meet his expectations. The family needed to establish more clearly defined rules that Jennie was prepared to follow, but it was not until Ian worked on repairing his relationship with Jennie and made a real effort to give her more praise and reassurance that she was able to move beyond her aggressive stance.

I am who I am

'He can't think for himself; he's got to do what his friends do all the time. They say "jump", he jumps,' complained Julie Hunt about Robert, her 15-year-old son. But for Robert the drinking, antisocial pranks and rule-breaking were all part of the thrill of belonging to a gang. 'I lead myself astray,' he laughed. 'My mum thinks it's my mates, but it's not just them.'

By taking up attitudes and behaviour that identified him with a particular peer group, Robert had stumbled across an easy solution to the much bigger challenge of working out who he was and where he wanted to go in life. In a sense, Julie and his stepfather David's frustration with his gang activities were playing into his hands: adults were *supposed* to find the group's behaviour threatening.

But there were other issues that needed facing in trying to help Robert establish a less destructive identity. In thinking about her reactions to his behaviour, Julie realized that she had been looking at Robert as a far younger child. Also, she had not previously thought about how he might have been affected by the relationship she had after divorcing his father (and before she met David), where Robert had tried to protect her from domestic violence. Robert was still getting into fights now, trying to protect other members of his gang, and Julie needed to tell him that it wasn't his job to adopt the role of protector – of her or his friends.

Julie was also able to use her own past to help Robert understand how his present identity could impact on his future. She revealed how her own waywardness as a teen had landed her in Borstal, and how it had taken intense focus on her goals to turn her life around. Helping Robert to confront the issue of his identity gave him a chance to take more responsibility for defining himself, rather than relying on the group identity offered by his gang.

Still my baby

Despite having had a leg operation, Sue Watts would be up and down the stairs to her son Suraj's bedroom with trays of food, alarm calls and even fruit on a little platter to ensure he ate his 'five-a-day fruit and veg'. Dominic and James Pauley's father John was still running around after his sons, putting out their clothes and making their beds long after the 15- and 13-year-old boys became capable of doing this for themselves. As a result, the boys were quite used to leaving their clothes on the floor and not tidying up their mess.

Some teenagers may find the responsibility of growing up so over-whelming that their behaviour is designed to make sure that they are always treated like children. But if you play along, you can make the problem worse. Sue was convinced that without her constant vigilance Suraj would come to some harm. While he may have welcomed the easy life at one level, Suraj was also being prevented from developing a capacity to look after himself. This can lead to resentment and confusion in teenagers who like to think of themselves as adults, but know that they still need to learn how to cope with adult life.

Queen of the world

Sixteen-year-old Anni Ellis was lively and sociable outside the house, but at home she was sulky and constantly at loggerheads with her mum Marie. 'When I ask her to do something, she always comes back with "Why? Why me?"' complained Marie. 'The arguments they have are over the most mundane, stupid things,' agreed dad, Chris.

But in reality, outside the home Anni was struggling. By challenging her parents to fiery shouting matches, she was compensating for some of the feelings of vulnerability she was experiencing because of her difficulty in keeping up at school. Teens with underlying fears about managing life in the adult world may try to reassure themselves by flexing their muscles, crashing through every boundary they encounter, and taking on authority wherever they find it.

By doing so, teenagers are trying to convince themselves that they are more powerful and adequate than they really feel deep down. If they can show that they have nothing to fear from anyone or anything, and prove themselves to be top dog in every situation, their illusion of power can be maintained. Like Anni, or Jennie Manson, who rowed constantly with her stepfather, there is a lot invested in never backing down. 'I've always got to be right – even if I know I'm wrong,' admitted Jennie.

By entering into these bouts of verbal sparring with her daughter, Marie was unknowingly allowing her daughter to avoid addressing her real problem. It was only when Anni's school started phoning and complaining about her attendance that the real problem was revealed.

Off their heads

Another solution for teenagers who feel threatened by the challenges of the outside world or just unable to cope with the turbulent feelings they have inside is to find ways to avoid such pressures altogether. They may do this by living for the moment, or becoming addicted to the 'rush' provided by activities such as vandalism, binge drinking, drugs or shoplifting. Robert Kingdon thought that his gang activities would 'take my mind off things' – in his case, the domestic violence he had witnessed in the past, as well as the fact that he was falling behind at school.

For teens who are committed to avoiding their inner demons, the stress of repeated and fruitless confrontations with their parents can add to the pressures they are seeking to escape. The result can be that they simply redouble their efforts to 'get out of their heads' by falling back on the very behaviour their parents are trying to reduce. Sixteen-year-old Tom Maddison recognized that he used cannabis to bury and soothe his underlying feelings of rage. Although cannabis is not physically addictive, Tom was one of a minority of users who develop a psychological dependency on the drug, and trying to stop smoking created further tension and pressure for him.

It is vital when dealing with this kind of behaviour to keep a cool head. Teens who use such methods to escape their problems need help to develop other ways of coping. If you allow yourself to become frantic with worry, or lash out in your own frustration, your teen is unlikely to see you as a safe person to confide in. He may also come to doubt that you are any better equipped to handle stress than he is. On the other hand, it is also important to give your teen a clear message about the limits of acceptable behaviour. There is more on this in Chapters 4 and 5.

The way you make me feel...

The stereotype of the inarticulate teen grunting his way through his adolescent years reflects how hard teenagers can find it to communicate what is really going on inside. Half the time they don't know themselves.

Sometimes teens stumble across a makeshift solution to this problem by using their own behaviour to make their parents feel the same way as they feel. Tom Maddison's behaviour provoked feelings of great anger in his parents: it was no surprise to discover that these were precisely the feelings Tom felt so intensely himself. Ian Manson felt only too clearly that Jennie's behaviour showed she didn't respect him. But it soon became evident that much of the time Jennie didn't feel respected either. Behaving badly was one way of projecting these feelings into those around her.

If your response to your teenager's behaviour confirms that this is the only way she can make herself understood, she is unlikely to develop more direct or constructive forms of communication. It is always worth asking yourself how your exchanges with your teenager leave you feeling. Do you recognize the emotions as ones your teen might relate to? In the next chapter we will show you how to respond differently to help your teen bridge the communication gap and restore better relations.

Breaking the cycle

In this chapter we have emphasized the benefits of thinking about and making adjustments to your own behaviour as a parent. But changing your behaviour means that you have got to examine some of your beliefs and assumptions, some of which might be very deep-seated. For some people, making this shift in thinking can be difficult.

If you interpret your teenager's rebellious behaviour as a malicious attempt to make your life a living hell, you will probably react very differently than if you decide that his behaviour is a 'cry for help' or a demonstration of how out of control he feels. And if you have negative expectations of your teenager, there's a danger that your expectations will simply feed the cycle of bad behaviour, thus creating a self-fulfilling prophecy.

'He's got so much potential, yet he's going to ruin all his chances,' said Sue Watts of Suraj. She felt unable to relax her constant vigilance and supervision of her son 'until he can show he's more responsible'. But this negative view was also propping up the bad behaviour. Sue's certainty that Suraj would go off the rails unless she intervened led to what he saw as constant nagging; in turn, Suraj lashed out against the nagging and continued to behave badly.

Similarly, Glynis and Rob Gibson had become so convinced that twins Jonny and Luke were impossible to discipline that they had given up trying. This meant that the twins' bad behaviour had just got worse and made them even more difficult to control.

Remember that sometimes it is necessary for parents to challenge their beliefs about themselves as well as about their teens. Helen Ryan saw herself as a mother who could never provide enough for her daughters Lucie and Elane, so she would over-compensate by going on spending sprees she could barely afford. It was not until she started to appreciate that her girls did value the consistent care, loyalty and affection she had shown them over the years that she began to feel confident enough to resist their boundless appetite for new clothes.

As these examples show, you need to break the cycle by thinking again. It may be very hard to believe the best of your teen when everything he is doing seems designed to make you think the worst. But part of your job as the parent of a teenager is to keep faith with your child, while his job is to test that commitment to the limit. Beneath the bravado teenagers can feel very insecure. Your teenager may be badly in need of your support if she is to find the confidence to let go of patterns of behaviour she has come to rely on.

Getting positive

The first step in breaking the vicious cycle is for you to try to notice the good things about your teen – however scarce they may appear, and even if they do seem overshadowed by the negative. This process will enable you to refocus and weaken your negative expectations of your child. With any luck, it will gradually become easier to notice the qualities about your child that are still lovable and admirable. This will create its own cycle of a different, more positive set of expectations. As your outlook becomes more positive, your teen will start to feel buoyed up by your determination to look on the good side – and you may be pleasantly surprised to find him increasingly able to live up to your better expectations.

❍ Spend a moment making a list of all the qualities you admire about your teen.

❍ Think about the last time you enjoyed spending time together. How did your son or daughter seem to you then?

❍ Look through some old photo albums and reconnect yourself with the sense of hope and promise that you felt about your child when she was younger.

❍ Think about yourself as a teenager and the personal journey you have made since those turbulent years.

❍ Paint a mental picture of a happy and positive future for your teenager in which the stresses of the present have been left behind. Statistically, the reality is that, however bad it seems now, most teenagers who cause their parents grief during these years do go on to become respectable, productive members of society.

It may be a good idea to keep a compliment book in which family members record things they appreciate about each other, or leave a note under your teenager's pillow to encourage her. By actively building up your teenager's self-esteem, you have a powerful opportunity to change both your attitude and hers, and the whole way in which you relate to each other.

One note of caution: your teenager may prove quite resistant at first. Some teens are very committed to their image of themselves as bad, unlovable kids, and may oppose your efforts to treat them otherwise. Some may be highly suspicious of this change in your approach. As a result, you may find that their behaviour gets worse before it improves. However, if you stick to your guns, few teenagers will ultimately be able to resist your sustained positive attention. At the very least, by changing your own perspective and being more positive you can improve the impact that their more difficult behaviour has on you.

You may not be able to force your teenager to change, but you can change yourself and your own behaviour. This is usually well worth doing. Your behaviour and attitudes have much more impact on your teenager than you probably realize.

POINTS TO REMEMBER

❍ Bad behaviour has both cause and effect. You will need to identify both if you want to combat it.

❍ Use your diary to learn to spot the triggers that produce unwanted behaviour.

❍ Look carefully at what happens when your teen behaves in undesirable ways. Become aware of the hidden goals driving your teen's behaviour to ensure that you are not encouraging behaviour you don't want.

❍ Common motivators may include:

- A need for attention – both positive and negative
- A desire for control and self-assertion
- A need for reassurance
- A desire to establish an identity
- An inability to communicate feelings
- A wish to avoid difficult feelings

❍ Your beliefs and attitudes will determine how you react. Try to challenge any negative expectations, as these can easily become a self-fulfilling prophecy.

chapter three

Shut up!

Mother: I'm just talking to you, Anni. Why does everything have to be like I'm accusing you? I'm not!
Daughter: Because mostly you are!

This exchange between 16-year-old Anni Ellis and her mother Marie highlights one of the main problems between parents and their children during the teenage years: communication. Nearly all teenagers complain that their parents don't understand them. But many parents of teenagers feel the reverse is equally true: that they just can't get through to their teens, let alone get them to listen to a parental point of view. Attempts to communicate either seem to fall on deaf ears, or break down in angry slanging matches. It's as if each character is following a different script – and feeling equally frustrated.

   The communication gulf that opens up during the teenage years can be truly daunting for both sides. Although most of the parents we met in *Teen Angels* were conscious that efforts to talk to their teenage children weren't working, they often had no idea how they could improve things. So perhaps the best place to start is with what doesn't work.

When it isn't working

There are a few key principles you can follow to help establish better communication in your family. By developing an awareness of the traps and pitfalls that can sabotage any relationship, you might be able to avoid some of the more frustrating stand-offs. This way both parent and teenager stand a better chance of getting what they want.

1 Show some respect

For Ian and Jennie Manson, months of arguing culminated in the ultimate breakdown in communication. One night, during a row over going out, 16-year-old Jennie swore at her stepdad, and he snapped. He reacted by slapping her round the face and then pinning her to the floor. The police were called, but no charges were pressed. Jennie had one or two bruises, but the real damage was to her feelings. Ian was unrepentant. 'If I'd walked away, she would have won,' he insisted. Later he tried to apologize, but Jennie was having none of it. 'I haven't got an ounce of respect for you,' Jennie said. Their relationship was in ruins.

What happened in the Manson family was extreme, but the behaviour that led to the fight is common. Jennie and her stepfather had created a way of communicating that left both parent and teen feeling attacked and humiliated. Jennie had developed a highly confrontational style, which in turn was driving Ian into more and more of a fighting mood. 'I don't like just giving up and backing down,' he said. Before long, a culture of aggression had been established in which meaningful communication had become virtually impossible. And what lay at the very root of the problem was a lack of respect.

People usually respond in one of two ways when they are verbally or physically attacked: fight or flight. It's an in-built, primitive response that means we either withdraw into wounded silence or storm out (flight), or strike back in verbal or physical ways that may inflame the situation (fight). Either response is likely to damage the prospect of genuine understanding. For this reason it is crucial to keep an eye on the way in which family members talk to each other, and to clamp down on any aspects of their communication that undermine a respectful attitude on either side.

Respect for a person does not include trying to control or manipulate him. Of course you still want your teenager to do what you ask, but think about how you can communicate in ways that will promote a culture of respect in the family, and help keep the channels open between you and your teen.

2 Stop shouting!

In the Parkinson/Ryan household shouting was the standard method of communication. Sisters Lucie and Elane were constantly yelling at each other and their mother Helen, and when they weren't shouting they were refusing to speak to each other. 'They grind you into the ground until you think, "I just don't care any more",' complained Helen. 'I think, "Go away and leave me to die".' Helen's description was dramatic, but in fact she was shouting just as much as her two shrieking daughters. It was almost impossible to work out when they were talking and when they were arguing, and the first strategy the psychologists insisted the family follow was to stop shouting.

If you resort to shouting, two things are usually true. First, you are trying to use sheer volume to dominate your opponent – literally trying to 'shout her down'. Second, when you shout you are actually broadcasting the message that you are losing control.

Your teenager may dislike you shouting at her on one level, but at the same time she may secretly enjoy her power to make you 'lose it'. It also gives her a good excuse to ignore whatever you're saying as you're not being 'reasonable'. It is important not to allow her this luxury.

It is also hard to respect someone who uses shouting as one of their regular communication strategies. However furious your teen's behaviour may leave you feeling, try to keep your cool when talking to him. He will be far more likely to accept what you have to say. You will also be showing him a more adult way of resolving conflict that doesn't involve being disrespectful.

On the other hand, if your teen is shouting at you, he has probably already passed the point at which reasoning with him is possible. It's better to bring the conversation to a halt before things reach this stage. There is no point in trying to communicate with a teenager who is in a rage or being verbally abusive. Your silence is likely to send a clearer message to him about about your disapproval than any attempt to talk him round.

Marie and Anni Ellis were both taken aback by footage of themselves shouting at each other on their behaviour tape. 'I'm horrified!' exclaimed Anni. 'I didn't know we sounded like that.' Mother and daughter were communicating plenty, but nearly always in hostile conditions. Sometimes they were even stirring up hostility as a way of getting some form of dialogue going.

Marie and Anni were taken through an exercise where they had to identify the thoughts that came into their heads the moment an argument started. Marie realized that she felt unappreciated and misunderstood by her daughter, while Anni felt that her mother took out all her frustrations on her. Yet by standing back and thinking about it they also realized that underneath it all they really had a lot of love and understanding for each other. They agreed that the moment they began to shout was actually the point of no return. They resolved to keep their voices calm and walk away as soon as possible if they spotted the signs that one of their explosive shouting matches was brewing.

3 You're not listening

'I want you to talk to me and listen to my point of view instead of using this as an opportunity to lay down rules and orders,' said Jennie Manson in the aftermath of her fight with her stepfather. You might find it difficult, but one of the most effective ways you can communicate respect for your teen is to listen carefully to what she has to say.

Studies have found that most people actually spend more time listening during communication than they do talking. But parents talking to their teens don't always follow this pattern: they seem to think they should be doing most of the talking. Conversations with teenagers often become battles for who can hold the floor and hammer their point of view across most forcefully.

The Parkinson family was given a new set of rules to follow in which mother Helen and her daughters Lucie and Elane had to speak to each other pleasantly every day, and to listen. If they started to argue, the rule was to listen to what the other person had to say and then walk away. Although the family found it hard to keep it up, the atmosphere in their house lifted almost immediately.

Listening is a skill that takes time to develop. It means paying attention while the other person speaks, and finding the right moment and
setting for a conversation to take place. David Hunt got frustrated with
his stepson Robert as he tried to talk to the teenager about his plans for
that evening while he was watching TV with a friend. Unsurprisingly,
Robert kept his eyes fixed on the screen and was slow to respond. This
wasn't unusual. During the making of *Teen Angels* we filmed people
trying to hold conversations as they read magazines, shouted at each
other from different rooms, kept one eye on the TV and even held a
simultaneous conversation with someone else on the phone.

Many people think that listening is a passive process, but it should
not be. You need to show your teenager that you are engaged by giving
signals, such as the occasional 'uh huh' or nod, and maintaining a good
level of eye contact. Your response lets your teen know that you are
paying attention to him, and taking his attempt to talk to you seriously.
Even more importantly, you should not interrupt to correct or criticize.

In order to listen you also need to accept that your teenager may
see things very differently from you. Teenagers often feel they are not
being taken seriously, and sometimes it is hard for them to express
what they feel. In view of this, it is especially important to cultivate
good listening skills. If you listen attentively to them, you can legiti-
mately expect the same in return when you have something to say.

However, if your teenager doesn't want to listen to you, it's probably not worth trying to talk to him. Sue Watts was so keen to pursue a discussion with Suraj about a college meeting that she followed
him into his room and sat on his bed while Suraj turned his back to
her, with headphones on, telling her repeatedly, 'I'm not listening, not
listening'. Sue's method of communication just wound up Suraj more,
and showed clearly that you can't *make* someone listen to you. In this
situation the best strategy is to withdraw and think again about how
and when to get your message across.

4 Mind your language

'You're f***ing grounded, Luke, and you know it,' Rob Gibson told his
15-year-old son after returning from a few days away at work. Luke

wouldn't have been offended by Rob's language, since he started every day himself by telling his mother to 'F*** off'. But in a family where the boys' mother felt unsupported in her attempts to control her sons, Rob's casual use of the same language was giving his sons the clear signal that it was acceptable to talk like that.

The language that we use can have a huge impact on the emotional tone of family life. Name-calling, swearing at each other, casual insults – even if done jokily or affectionately – can all send powerful signals about what is acceptable and how members of the family see each other. Even a casual remark about the way a teenager looks, particularly about body shape, can trigger insecurity and affect confidence.

In the Taylor family abusive talk was the norm. The family had got so used to speaking to each other rudely that they no longer noticed what they sounded like. Yet there was a constantly unpleasant atmosphere in the house and a mounting level of verbal aggression. Each member of the family was therefore encouraged to make a list of the names and phrases that they particularly disliked, and to share their lists with each other. The family had to follow a new rule: whenever they felt like using one of the names on the list, they were to substitute the phrase 'You are my sunshine' instead. It may sound silly, but this lighthearted approach helped the family to recognize how much they were winding each other up with their insulting remarks, and helped dispel some of the aggression in the house.

5 You always do this!

Below is an exchange that took place between 17-year-old Lucie Parkinson and her mother Helen when Lucie arrived home at 1.30 after a night out in town.

Lucie: (standing in doorway) I'm going to bed.
Helen: You're out of order, Lucie! You're way out of order. What time did I say? You should be in before one o'clock.
Lucie: I texted you when I got in the taxi.
Helen: Did you not understand what I said last week?
Lucie: Yeah, I did, but you didn't understand what I said either.

Helen: This is my house! You are not 18, and if I have to go down to the clubs [to get you], I will. You went out about twenty to ten.

Lucie: I didn't! It was nine o' clock.

Helen: No. I know exactly what time it was. Do you want me to ring the taxi company and check the log? It was twenty to ten.

Lucie: Why do you have to ring everybody anyway?

Helen: Because you tell me that I'm wrong and I know!

Lucie: (storming out) You're always right and I'm always wrong! That's always the way.

Helen: No, Lucie, that's not the case.

Lucie: It is always the way, Mum.

Although there was clearly disagreement about what time Lucie should come home, this was not a model for successful communication with a teenager. By arguing over the facts rather than their feelings about the situation, Lucie and her mother ended up locking horns in a way that was bound to end in communication meltdown. Their conversation simply became a power struggle in which each party tried to wrestle the other into agreement with their version of events.

It is not surprising that Lucie put up such a fight because Helen's account placed her daughter in such a negative light. The implication of Helen's words was that Lucie was rebellious ('You're out of order'); immature ('You are not 18'); and a liar ('I know exactly what time it was'). Helen's tone was accusing and judgemental, and Lucie's was angry and defensive, eventually becoming accusing in return.

Nobody likes being judged or told what they are like by someone else, and teens can be particularly sensitive about this since they are often struggling to define themselves already. Your teenager is better placed to know what is going on inside her head and heart than you are, meaning that your unwelcome interpretations and judgements are likely to be challenged and resisted at every turn. What Helen needed to do was speak more forthrightly of her own feelings about the situation, rather than launching accusations against her daughter.

When things get heated the proportion of accusations can often increase: '*You* seem to think money grows on trees'; '*You* are so irresponsible these days'; 'You don't care about anyone but yourself'. However, consider the difference between the following statements:

'**You** are so unreliable and selfish. **You** think you can come and go as you please without a thought for anyone else. **You** are completely untrustworthy.'

'**I** was hurt and upset when you didn't come in at the time we had agreed. **I** want to be able to trust you, but your behaviour makes that difficult for **me** at the moment.'

The first example focuses on the teen and makes a series of negative generalizations about the teenager's character and attitudes. In the second the parent is focusing on his own feelings. Even the most argumentative teen is in no position to challenge your immediate experience.

Helen was understandably tired and annoyed after waiting up until 1.30 for Lucie, especially knowing that she had school the next day. But what she might have said to Lucie was: 'I'm disappointed that you haven't done what I asked and come in before one o' clock. I know that you don't agree with this time, but I would like you to stick to it rather than texting me when it was already too late. It is difficult for me to trust you if you do not stick to our agreement.'

6 Don't go on

'I just blank it because she utters a load of rubbish… I'm just like, "Yeah, yeah, yeah… Totally agree, Mum!"' Fifteen-year-old Jonny Gibson had got so used to his mother Glynis nagging him that he took no notice of anything she had to say. He'd learnt how to deflect her either by ignoring her or by swearing. Meanwhile, the less impact Glynis felt she had, the more she felt she had to nag, particularly first thing in the morning when her twin boys refused to get up. 'If I didn't say anything, they'd just lie there,' she insisted.

Parents often fall into the trap of nagging in the desperate hope that if they go on enough, they might force their teenagers to acknowledge their point of view or just give in. Of course, most teenagers are neither stupid nor deaf. They're usually going to hear you the first time, even if they don't show it. But as soon as your teenager perceives your frustration, he will often dig his heels in and let you slowly transform yourself into such a nag that he can justifiably ignore you. Just as a toddler senses that he can become more powerful by not responding to your requests straight away, so teens often adopt a similar strategy.

The most vital piece of advice to hold on to when communicating with your teenager is simple: keep it brief. Say what you have to say, then stop – however tempting it may be to keep going.

Sue Watts had got so concerned about her son Suraj's late-night partying and poor performance at college that she felt she couldn't stop nagging him. But Suraj was so infuriated by this that he could barely look at her, let alone communicate. 'I feel completely helpless,' she said. 'I keep thinking, "What can I say that is going to be more effective?"' But she also felt justified in going on. 'I can't relax this until he can show he's more responsible,' she declared.

If you feel you must endlessly justify your position like this, you will make yourself look weak and your teen will take advantage. Every time Sue started nagging, Suraj would either shout at her, walk out or give her a withering look known to the family as 'the face of disgust'. It's better simply to make your point, give a clear reason why and let your teen know that you're willing to discuss it further if he wishes. Don't get drawn into pleading or fruitless lectures that will lead nowhere.

Sue was asked to say what she needed to say to Suraj once and once only, giving him the opportunity to take more responsibility for the things he needed to do without her nagging. But when Suraj still failed to do what she asked him to do, such as tidying up and not smoking in his room, Sue needed to introduce consequences. Having clear consequences set in place cuts across the need for endless accusations and debates. A teen learns far more effectively from experiencing the consequences of her own actions than from repeated telling off. We will show you how to create effective boundaries and consequences in Chapter 5.

7 Don't play mind games

It's very tempting when you're feeling irritated to resort to a variety of power-play strategies to outwit or wrong-foot your teen. You might be trying to get the upper hand, perhaps extort a confession, or even 'trick' the teen into agreeing that you're in the right. But this can often backfire, as teenagers can be just as skilful at these kinds of game. All you're really doing is encouraging them to wind you up too. The best way to talk to your teen is one that is open, honest and direct.

AVOIDABLE WIND-UPS

Twenty questions: Resist the temptation to interrogate your teen with a barrage of questions in the hope that you will be able to pin him down and force him to acknowledge his guilt. Teenagers particularly hate it if you ask questions to which you already know (or believe you know) the answer. As Suraj said angrily to his mother, 'Why are you asking me if you already know what you think?' He had a point.

Digging up the past: Don't rake up past misdemeanours as evidence to hold against your teen for a current problem, especially if she has already apologized and made amends for crimes past. Most teens will be infuriated by any attempt to revisit old incidents, particularly if they have already 'done the time' by accepting a punishment.

Guilt-tripping: 'Why can't you do this little thing for me?' Sue asked Suraj. He'd told her he was going to an all-night party, and she wanted the phone number of where he was going. Although it was not unreasonable to ask him to leave a contact number, the way Sue went about it just made Suraj dig in his heels even further. 'It's not only you,' she pleaded. 'What if something happens to me?'

There is a difference between being honest with your teen in a matter-of-fact way about how his behaviour has affected you, and deliberately exploiting your distress as a way of controlling or punishing him. Parents who play the victim role or use lines such as, 'Can't you see what you're doing to your poor mother?' are likely to get an unsympathetic response. Although teens may feel free to push their own feelings of anger, discomfort and insecurity on to you, they don't like this sort of tactic being turned against them. Your child is not responsible for your emotional well-being, and it will damage your relationship if you try to force this upon him.

Negative comparisons: There's nothing more irritating for a teenager than being compared to friends, siblings, other people's children, or even yourself. It's as if you're holding up a mirror to her in which she can only appear inadequate. She will also feel that your comparisons are irrelevant: like all teens, she wants to be considered an individual in her own right. Also, when you start comparing you stop empathizing. Your teen is likely to sense your disengagement and steel herself to resist you.

It is also very easy for siblings to feel labelled as the 'good' or 'bad' child within families. Your teenager may feel this is a form of prejudice that she is unable to fight, and it may also encourage her to fulfil your prophecy that she is 'bad'. Fourteen-year-old Gemma Taylor was convinced that her parents thought her 16-year-old brother Roy could do no wrong, while she was the bad kid. Consequently, she lived up to the prophecy by being aggressive and getting into trouble at school.

HOW TO AVOID ARGUMENTS

❍ Don't speak to your child in a way that may cultivate a climate of disrespect, and don't allow her to do so either.

❍ Don't shout – it shows you are not in control.

❍ Learn to listen to what your teen has to say, even if you don't like what he's saying.

❍ Don't accept bad language or verbal abuse, even as a joke.

❍ Don't tell your teenager what she's like. If you want to show that you are unhappy with her behaviour, focus instead on how you are feeling about it.

○ Don't nag. Make your point briefly and leave it at that.
○ Don't bombard your teenager with questions.
○ Don't guilt-trip or make comparisons to others.
○ Don't drag up the past at every opportunity. Learn to move on.

How to improve communication

If you want to establish successful communication with your teenager, the best strategy is to build him up rather than put him in his place. Of course there are going to be many times when you are annoyed with him, but if you can keep the tone of your conversation constructive and positive, it will be better for both of you.

1 Rewrite your script

Fights between parents and teenagers often have a surprisingly predictable, ritualistic quality to them. It is as if everyone is working to a set script of how they should react and even what they should say. The content of the arguments may change, but the outward form tends to remain the same: the invisible script relies on the parent and teen playing the same old familiar roles each time. If you can work out the script and understand the pattern of the dance that your family may be stuck in, you've got a much better chance of breaking the cycle.

We all occupy a number or roles in our dealings with others, and these may not bear any relation to our age or position in the family. Sixteen-year-old Roy Taylor had adopted the role of an authoritarian parent figure, barking orders at his mother Dawn. Despite herself, Dawn would often end up slipping into a submissive, child-like role, and allow him to shout abuse at her, order her around and tell her to 'get out of my room'. Without realizing it, she had taken a role that complemented the one taken by Roy.

Dawn had to learn ways of rewriting the script so that they could communicate in a completely different way. In fact, the whole family had got so used to speaking to her in an aggressive way that they had almost stopped noticing when they were being rude to her. Imagine their surprise when one day Dawn produced a whistle, gave a piercing blast and announced, 'I don't deserve to be treated like this' in a firm voice before marching out of the room. She was taking on a new role. From then on, if anyone was rude to her, she would go and sit down for ten minutes and read a magazine. The message was clear: if she wasn't treated with respect, she would withdraw.

Similarly, Glynis Gibson used to switch between two roles – one in which she nagged and provoked twin sons Luke and Jonny, and a second in which she would constantly give in to them. When she changed her own script to become calmer and clearer she was able to put consequences into effect for their swearing and lashing out at her. Although Jonny was still very abusive when Glynis tackled him about his behaviour, she managed to do so without shouting or nagging, and didn't sink to Jonny's level as she had done so often in the past. Consequently she stayed in control.

The roles that we assume in relation to our teenagers are often conditioned by our own experiences of growing up. Many parents will have had the chilling experience of hearing statements come out of their mouths that echo their own mother or father, even if they've been determined not to parent in the same way. Don't underestimate how automatically some of these roles can be cued, or how good teenagers can be at activating them. You might want to consider the following questions:

○ What are the roles I seem to end up playing time and again in my conversations with my teen?

○ What are the values that lie behind these roles? Do I agree with them?

○ What past experiences make it easy for me to fall into these roles?

○ What do they stop me from expressing?

○ When I adopt these roles, how does my teenager respond? What roles does she assume in return?

○ How could we break out of our pattern? If I was acting 'out of character', what would I be doing differently?

2 Get off on the right foot

When Helen Ryan got back late from the launderette, she burst in, shouting at top volume for her daughters Lucie and Elane, who had been snoozing in front of the fire. Her yelled instructions – 'Take your own stuff! Just say what's yours – don't throw them in a heap!' – quickly drew her daughters into an escalating fight, and before long everyone was shouting at each other. Helen was busy of course, and wanted the washing sorted quickly, but not being able to take a step back and gauge her daughters' mood meant that she quickly provoked them.

The attitude you convey at the beginning of a communication is likely to determine how well it goes. If you burst in with all guns blazing, there's a good chance that your teenager will react in a similar way. If there's more hostility than praise or attention in the way you communicate, the atmosphere will be hostile. Always try to get off on the right foot before making demands or giving instructions.

3 Say what you want

Try to let your teen know what you do want, rather than pulling him up constantly on the behaviour you don't want. 'I would like you to hang the towel up when you have used it' stands a much better chance of getting the right response than 'I can't believe you've just left the towel in a sopping heap on the floor – again!'

4 Give positive feedback

Coming from a strict military background, Ian Manson saw compliments as something that had to be earned. 'If you don't do anything over and above what you're supposed to do, you've done nothing,' he insisted. Yet his 16-year-old stepdaughter Jennie felt conscious of his lack of praise for her. 'When he does say "Well done", it's always followed by "You can do better",' she complained.

Ian and his wife Tina needed to make up a bird table from a flat pack. They were asked to include Jennie and let her take charge, making sure they gave her lots of compliments and positive feedback. Ian thought that he would find this difficult to do, but as soon as he got into the swing of saying nice things to Jennie he saw an immediate reaction. She began smiling and laughing, literally 'glowing with praise'. It was proof that they could communicate well, and the atmosphere between them began to lift.

Even if you find it hard to come up with something positive to comment on, it does work if you can encourage your teen. Make sure you give him positive feedback when he does behave well or do something that has pleased you. Teens may appear resistant to compliments, but will usually appreciate them deep down. Sometimes a written note left on a pillow or pinned to a door may be more acceptable to your teen if he feels embarrassed by praise given in person.

5 Keep faith

However bad your teenager has been, it's important to keep a distinction between the behaviour that you find unacceptable and the child you still love. If the behaviour is labelled as bad, you are signalling that there is scope for change. However, if the teen is labelled as bad, you are implying something very different, and painting a bleak picture of the future for both of you.

Even if you are disciplining your teen, it's important to make it clear that he is still a good, capable person whom you believe will ultimately make good choices in his life, despite the mistakes of the present. When Julie Hunt needed to punish her son Robert for staying out all night without her permission, she practised the new communication skills she had learnt. She told Robert that she was unhappy with his actions, and that she was going to ground him. She didn't shout or scream, and made it clear that her feelings about him hadn't changed. As soon as she had communicated what she needed to, she quickly moved on.

6 Keep engaging

It's harder to find things that you can do with teenagers than it is with young children, but it's important to find ways of spending time together if you want to keep the channels of communication open. When Rob Gibson was asked to take his twin sons bowling, it revealed some of the problems he had in relating to them, particularly Luke.

Rob found it difficult to engage his sons in conversation or to tell them that they were doing well, and Luke became easily discouraged by his father's lack of approval or praise. Luke's way of dealing with this was to cold-shoulder his father when he tried to talk to him. Rob was shown that he needed to work on having conversations with Luke to draw him in. Although the teenager was giving off the signal that he didn't want to know, it just took a little persistence to get him engaged. Without the opportunity to spend time together, there would have been less likelihood that they would have started talking.

After a lot of conflict, Sue Watts and Suraj spent an afternoon painting china. It seemed an unlikely way for them to relax together, but away from the pressures of normal life, Sue was able to ask simple questions rather than give advice or nag. Without an agenda of her own to pursue, she was also able to listen to his answers. As a result, Suraj responded in an easygoing manner. He even revealed the source of some of his problems: he'd been having girl trouble.

With parents often busy working, and teenagers either at school or out with friends, it can be hard to find the right opportunity to discover if things are going well. Try to find a little time to spend together each week away from the stresses and strains of the usual routine. Your teenager may not have anything to tell you, but it will create a space for her to do so if she needs to.

7 Help them tell you what's wrong

Helen Ryan was understandably annoyed when her daughter Elane suddenly declared that she didn't want to go to the Busted concert for which Helen had bought tickets several weeks previously. But as is often the case with teenagers, what you see on the surface isn't always the whole story. If Helen had been able to communicate better with Elane, she might have discovered that Elane had fallen out with some of her friends and was feeling so low that she had made herself sick. Instead, Elane cried secretly in her room, while she was outwardly aggressive towards her mum about not wanting to go.

8 Help them find their own solutions

Try to maintain the distinction between offering support and offering advice. While it's important for your teenager to be able to tell you if he is having problems, it's vital that you empower him to come up with his own solutions. It might be tempting to try to rescue him by offering solutions straight away, especially as you may feel that this is a rare occasion for you to get your opinion across. You may even feel flattered that he still values your opinion. But part of your job as the parent of a teenager is to help your child find his own solutions to life's problems. This is a skill he will need to develop along the road to becoming an adult.

Rather than responding to the part of your child that wants rescuing, it is usually more helpful to cast yourself in the role of an understanding mentor who helps your child find his own answers by asking the right questions. Try the following approach:

○ Encourage him to talk you through the situation and explore the options as he sees them while you listen.

○ Draw your child out by asking relevant questions that might highlight the advantages and disadvantages of any likely solutions.

○ Offer your own thoughts and perspectives only when you have followed the previous step.

○ Share your ideas to come up with a list of workable solutions together.

○ Look back at your list and agree on a way forward. You can assess this again over the weeks to come.

POINTS TO REMEMBER

○ The best communication strategy is to build your teen up rather than put him in his place.

○ Think about the roles you play within the family, and the script you follow, and rewrite if necessary.

○ Always start a communication as you would like it to continue – open and positive.

○ Let your teenager know what you want.

○ Give as much positive feedback as you can to the things your child is doing well.

○ Have faith, and let your teen know that your essential feelings towards him haven't changed, even if you are obviously unhappy with his behaviour.

○ Find ways of engaging your teen, and opportunities where you can talk and listen.

○ Help her to find ways of telling you when things are wrong.

○ Help her to find her own ways of solving problems.

chapter four

Whose life is it anyway?

WHEN 15-YEAR-OLD ROBERT KINGDON AND HIS PARENTS JULIE AND DAVID HUNT SAT down to watch his behaviour tape no one was happy. His parents were shocked to see Robert down at the local recreation ground, smoking, drinking and being unruly. Even worse was the pack mentality of Robert and his 'hoodied' friends, repeatedly kicking the door of the local youth club until the police were called. The combination of seeing this behaviour and receiving letters from the school about fighting and poor performance meant a lot of worry.

But Robert was equally horrified when he saw footage of his parents in his bedroom searching his school bag. His stepfather was looking for evidence of drug-taking; his mother was checking his work and trying to find out whether he was hiding more letters from school. Trust between parents and teen was at an all-time low.

R is for responsibility

David and Julie's actions reflected how frustrating it can be parenting a teenager. As your child approaches adulthood, it stands to reason that he should be taking more responsibility for his own life. But it's difficult to see how when he's also indulging in highly irresponsible behaviour.

Nor is it easy to raise the issue of responsibility. When David tried to find out why Robert hadn't called to say he wouldn't be home on time one Friday night, Robert said he'd had no credit on his phone, ignoring the fact that he was allowed to reverse the charges. David suggested that a little more responsibility wouldn't hurt. What he didn't hear was Robert parodying him saying the word 'responsibility', or the expletive muttered once he'd turned his back. Robert was typical of many teens: eager to assert his rights to greater freedom, but seemingly reluctant to take on the responsibilities that make such freedoms possible.

Faced with this sort of behaviour, many parents of teens naturally end up trying to take back control. The bad behaviour in turn reinforces the belief that if the parents don't keep their teenager on a tight rein, he is going to mess up. Unfortunately, this attitude may only encourage the teenager to view himself as incompetent, which may in turn reduce the likelihood of his behaving more responsibly.

So how do you decide when to intervene and when to stand back and let your teenager face the consequences of his own choices? It may seem an alien thought, but what parents often need to do is start to think about themselves more. You need to take more responsibility for yourself and the protection of your own happiness. Doing so will help you identify the areas where you need to take assertive action, while releasing you from the thankless task of trying to run your teenager's life.

Stand up for your rights

A baby cannot look after herself and relies on her parents to do so. Being a conscientious parent means taking complete responsibility for her well-being, and probably making many personal sacrifices along the way. As she grows and matures, the relationship between you should become more balanced. She can begin to do more things for herself, and take more responsibility.

That's the theory at least. In reality, by the time many children reach their teenage years their parents have often become so used to focusing on the children's needs that they have learnt to neglect their own. They fail to appreciate that the ground rules have changed and that they are entitled to expect more from their teen than from a younger child. The parents' sense of well-being continues to be determined by the state of their child's life, even though they have increasingly less control over the kind of choices their teen is making. This can be a recipe for unhappiness, as Sue Watts discovered.

'The moment he was born I just fell in love with him,' Sue said of her son Suraj. Now he was 16, testing her at every turn, swearing, smoking in the house and failing at school. But Sue was unable to let go of Suraj, and was unable to see that he had to begin to take responsibility for his own actions. She needed help to see that the best way she could help her son learn was through his own mistakes. If she was always there with him, following his every move, he would never begin to take responsibility, and she would never stop worrying.

But Sue had also lost sight of the fact that Suraj was treating her and husband Phil terribly. He came in late with little regard for how much noise he made, blatantly defied her requests not to smoke in the house, ran up the phone bill, treated Sue like a housemaid and swore at her in front of his friends. Suraj had no regard for his parents' rights.

The best way of showing your teenager that you accept he is becoming an adult is by insisting that your relationship now needs to be conducted on a more equal basis. That means your own needs, rights and feelings being taken into account just as much as his. Following this principle should help clarify which aspects of your teen's behaviour you need to tackle, and which you're prepared to let go.

Spend a few moments thinking about yourself, beyond your role as a parent. What do you need? What do you deserve? Are you getting it? Does the very idea of having rights seem alien to you after so many years of parenting? Spend a few moments with a pen and paper jotting down what you would like your own personal bill of rights to be. It might include ideas like those below.

MY BILL OF RIGHTS
I deserve:
○ Not to be insulted or abused
○ Not to be taken advantage of
○ Not to be a doormat
○ To be treated respectfully in my own home
○ To pursue my personal happiness

Now consider how many of the difficulties you are experiencing with your teen involve some violation of the rights you have listed. Would you tolerate the same treatment from anyone else?

Many parents are bad at defending their rights. But if you don't learn to do so, you are likely to end up feeling depressed, powerless and unappreciated. People in this state can be miserable to live with, and are likely to end up responding in ways that just make the situation worse.

'I'm bullied at times, I've definitely felt that,' said Lesley Maddison Stokes of her life in a house with two stroppy teenage boys. 'I've felt the dread of coming home.' She realized that she was letting 16-year-old Tom in particular push her around – mostly verbally – but there were times when she was beginning to feel a physical threat from him. Lesley learnt that she needed to take a much tougher stance on considering her own needs when Tom was making aggressive demands of her. This helped her stick to her guns and ask Tom to leave home when his behaviour became too threatening.

If you do not stand up for your rights, you also risk setting a bad example for your teen, who may learn to imitate your passive behaviour. Most parents want their sons and daughters to stand up for themselves. They also want them to treat other people well. Parents undermine both these aims when they allow their teenage children to walk all over them.

Tina Manson was upset when Jennie had a fight with her friends in the garden of the house. There was a lot of shouting and swearing, furniture was broken and Tina felt threatened. Afterwards Jennie was angry that the family wouldn't leave her alone when they could see she was still in a fury. But Tina needed to stand up for her own rights by getting Jennie to understand how upsetting the incident had been for her. 'It's not about you!' was Jennie's response. Tina needed to confront Jennie and explain to her that she felt hurt, unvalued and upset about the broken things. Eventually Jennie apologized.

Whose problem is it?

Have a look back through your diary and remind yourself of the main areas where your teenager's behaviour is currently causing you concern. Once you have identified the problem areas, ask yourself the following two questions about each problem:

○ How does the problem behaviour affect my teenager?
○ How does the problem behaviour affect me?

Sometimes it can be difficult to tease out the different implications for each side. But what you should end up with is two separate lists. We have used Sue Watts' problems with her son Suraj as an example, showing how she might have broken down those problems under two different headings.

PROBLEMS AND THEIR EFFECTS

Problem	List A How it affects my teenager	List B How it affects me
Suraj's room is a mess.	• He will end up living in squalor. • His friends may think he is a slob. • He may end up having an equally lax approach to other areas of his life.	• Dirty mugs in his room means there are none when I need them. • Dirty plates and washing lying around make my house unsanitary. • I have to pick up all the washing to make sure it gets done.
Suraj is smoking in the house.	• He is putting himself at risk of life-threatening disease. • Smoking is expensive and will eat into his money. • All his things will smell of smoke.	• I hate the smell of smoke. • I am worried that he may be smoking cannabis. I have a legal responsibility not to allow drugs to be used in my house. • I worry that he may start a fire if he falls asleep while smoking.
Suraj is on a final warning from the college.	• He may be thrown out, jeopardizing his A levels. • Without qualifications, he may not get the job he wants. • He is wasting his potential.	• I will be disappointed if he doesn't do as well as he could, but it isn't going to affect my life.

By breaking down each behaviour in this way you can start to think about what you can change and what you can't. We suggest that you concentrate your efforts on tackling the problems in List B – in other words, target the ways in which your teen's behaviour is affecting *your* life. Increasingly, you should then be able to hand back responsibility for List A problems to your teen.

There are several advantages to doing this. First, by making this distinction you give yourself a clear rationale for acting. Many teenagers will defend their right to live in a tip in their own space, but few will contest your right to find a clean mug in the cupboard when you need one. Second, by breaking the problems down into these distinct areas, you are clarifying what needs to be done.

In the case of Suraj's room, Sue's list didn't need the room to be spotlessly tidy. But what she did want was crockery brought downstairs, no dirty mugs or old food left around, and all dirty washing to be put in the laundry basket. Suraj quickly saw the advantage of doing this. 'I've brought my stuff down so I can be left unbothered in my room for half an hour,' he laughed.

In the second example it was clear that trying to ban Suraj from smoking wasn't going to work: it's impossible to police what your teenager does outside the house. However, the smoking at home was affecting Sue because she hated the smell and was worried about the fire hazard. So she insisted that Suraj no longer smoked in the house. She was also concerned that he might be smoking cannabis in his room, and made it clear that if she suspected he was doing so, she would search his room and confiscate it. Again, she couldn't necessarily stop him from doing it, but she could insist it didn't happen under her roof.

By adopting this teen-problem/parent-problem approach you are conserving your energy to tackle the problems that affect you directly, concentrating on the areas you can control, and encouraging your teen to take responsibility for the areas you can't. The third example highlights one area of Suraj's behaviour over which Sue couldn't have much influence. She could give Suraj as much encouragement as possible to keep on track at college, but ultimately if he was going to fail at school, that was going to be his problem.

When you've made your list and are thinking about the way forward with your own List B problems, remember that it's important to give your teen an opportunity to make her own suggestions. Problem-solving together can often generate fresh and practical solutions to longstanding grievances, and she may be prepared to give more ground than you expected.

However, if your teen still refuses to play ball, you can put in place sanctions to ensure that the List B problems are resolved. When Suraj stopped picking up his dirty washing, Sue decided to bag everything in bin liners and lock them away so that he had no clothes to go out in. When he still smoked in his room, she stopped buying him any treats, such as muffins or crisps. This was her way of showing that she wasn't going to be a doormat. There is more on choosing appropriate and effective sanctions in the next chapter.

Have your say

We are not suggesting that just because some aspects of your teen's behaviour may affect him more than you that you should not express your opinion about them. If you have concerns about *any* issue that could affect your child's well-being, you need to talk it through. Do remember, though, that teenagers will often respond better if you keep your comments focused on your own feelings about the situation and avoid taking back responsibility or control. They need to feel that they still are in charge.

Thirteen-year-old James Ellis was often in trouble at school for not completing his homework, and his parents were worried. His mother Marie would constantly remind him that his homework needed to be done, and didn't always believe him when he told her he'd done it. So she would secretly check up on James by searching through his bag to sneak a look at his homework diary, and find out whether he'd got any detentions. James was outraged when he saw footage of her searching through his bag, and felt that she'd invaded his privacy.

James's performance at school was a particular source of worry to Marie. She felt that she wasn't doing her job as a parent if she didn't ask him about it, but James experienced Marie's concern as an attempt to control him and was digging his heels in.

Although they were nervous about doing so, Marie and husband Chris were encouraged to hand responsibility for doing homework back to James and let him face the consequences at school if the work wasn't done. When they sat down to discuss it with him they followed this plan.

○ First they needed to outline the problem, from their own point of view:

'We are really worried that you are getting into trouble for not doing your homework properly.'

○ Then they pointed out what this could mean for James:

'Our concern is that if you don't do your homework, you will fall behind at school, fail to get the grades you need and that this may stop you from getting the kind of job you want.'

○ They had to let James know that only he could take responsibility for this problem:

'At the end of the day we cannot make you do your homework, and you are old enough to make this decision for yourself.'

○ They showed that they were still there to support and help James, and that they had faith that he would make the right choice:

'We'll do anything we can to help you, but we trust you to do the right thing, which is why we're leaving it in your hands.'

Chris and Marie also went to see James's teachers to let them know that they were now adopting this approach on a trial basis. The school agreed and gave James a month's deadline to turn his work around. His initial response was 'That's a bit crap', but he did in fact knuckle down and take a more responsible approach to what he needed to do.

Exceptions to the rule

There are some situations in which you may have a responsibility to try to intervene, even if the problem concerned is one that affects mostly your teen. If your teenager is at risk of harming herself or others, has developed a serious eating disorder, or is showing symptoms of mental illness or criminal behaviour, you can't afford to stand by. A teenager behaving in any of these ways is letting you know that she is currently incapable of taking much responsibility for herself. She is already feeling out of control.

Even if your teenager insists that she has the problem in hand or is reluctant to allow you to help, you may need to take advice from your GP or Social Services to try to ensure that your teen gets the professional help she needs.

However, you may also have to acknowledge that your power to do anything is limited. In certain situations, if your teen is still of sound mind, the most you can probably do is persuade her to recognize her need for help. You will have to be sensitive, as too heavy-handed an approach may result in your teen becoming even more firmly entrenched in the problem.

Ultimately, if your teen consistently refuses your help, you may have little option but to take a firm line and attend to the part of the problem you can control: the impact that your teen's behaviour is having on you and other family members.

'All I can see for Tom at the moment is sleeping in a shop doorway with a blanket and dog,' said Lesley Maddison Stokes. Life was going badly wrong for Tom. His dope smoking was becoming a daily habit; his parents' attempts to get him to take responsibility for his actions by giving him a weekly allowance in return for household chores had failed. Tom had previously told his parents that he was cutting down his cannabis use, and that he was seeing a drugs counsellor. But he was clearly unable to manage his money on a weekly basis, and was spending it all on drugs. As a result, his behaviour was getting more out of hand, and his aggression was beginning to frighten his parents.

Realizing that Tom was threatening the well-being of the family with his drug-taking and aggression, Lesley had to make the toughest decision of all and ask him to leave. Ultimately, because Tom needed to help himself, Lesley had no option but to prioritize her own rights and those of the rest of the family. 'I never ever dreamt in a million years that I would end up throwing my own child out,' she said. 'But I'm taking charge of my own life again, because I haven't been in charge of it for a long time.'

Encourage responsibility

There are several ways in which you can help your teenager to develop a sense of responsibility.

1 Resist the urge to supervise

'I feel churned up inside...to me I'm letting people down,' said Glynis Gibson. It was the first morning that she had left her sons to get themselves up. Luke had failed to get up in time and had missed his lift to school. It was hard for Glynis, but it was a vital step in showing the boys that they were responsible for themselves from now on.

Glynis was told to call the boys once, make sure they were awake, and leave the rest to them. Don't hover over your teenagers when they need to fulfil their responsibilities. Take a deep breath and let them get on with it. If necessary, create a clear deadline by which the task is to be completed and then assess the performance. Be clear and specific about what you expect, but don't protect your teenagers from the consequences of their actions.

2 Give responsibility at home

There's no reason why a healthy teenager should need to be entirely looked after by her parents any more. Part of the progression towards a more balanced relationship is the message that everyone is expected to pull their weight around the home. All teenagers should be helping with household chores, looking after their own belongings, picking up their dirty laundry and helping to tidy up.

Linking chores to getting an allowance is a great way of emphasizing the law of cause and effect in a way that most teens can quickly grasp. Tom and Nick Maddison's agreement with their parents involved taking on more domestic chores: they would clean the bathrooms and hoover the downstairs every week by Saturday lunchtime, as well as tidy their rooms and change their sheets. In return they would get their weekly allowance. Fifteen-year-old Nick found this worked well for him. 'I'm getting more responsibility with the money, and they've started treating me more like an adult,' he said.

3 Give feedback

'I don't know if my mum and dad have seen that I've been trying, because I have,' said Jennie Manson. 'If I come in on time it's just, "Oh, hello".' Jennie was discovering that behaving well can sometimes attract less attention than behaving badly. For that reason it's important to notice and be complimentary when your teen does honour her responsibilities. It can be frustrating if her responsible behaviour is taken for granted and only irresponsible behaviour gets attention.

If your teen is behaving in ways you don't like, it's important to let her know that too. One of the natural consequences of irresponsible behaviour is that the people around you become distressed and angry. You should not shield your teen from the fact that her behaviour provokes strong feelings in you, but remember to report your feelings without trying to use them to manipulate her.

4 Support your child's search for identity

A lot of the behaviour that gets labelled 'irresponsible' comes from teenagers who have yet to develop a very clear sense of who they are or where they are going in life. Exposing your son or daughter to a range of experiences and opportunities that may help them learn more about themselves and what motivates them can make all the difference.

When Helen Ryan went to Disneyland Paris with her two teenage daughters in a large coach group, she was furious that the girls broke away from the group and had a good time together on their own. She denounced their behaviour as 'selfish'. But the girls were exploring their independence and enjoying being together, and this was something that they needed to do. Helen was emotionally punishing them for quite normal teenage behaviour.

'Out-of-control' teen Gemma Taylor started helping out at a local nursery school, and the experience revealed a whole new side to her character. A trip to a forensic science laboratory at a local university also helped her to think about the future and why it might be worth taking her education more seriously.

5 Lead by example

With their hypersensitive nose for fair play, teens will instantly detect if you are asking them to behave in ways that you don't live up to. That's why Rob Gibson swearing at his sons when he wanted them to stop swearing at their mother was not going to work.

Never underestimate the power of your own example. Even if your teenager appears completely indifferent to you, he will be watching your every move. If you lead by example, he'll see the benefits of making responsible choices in his own life.

6 Let them own their successes and their failures

Tom Maddison was hugely proud of the fact that even though many things were going wrong for him, he had managed to earn the money to buy a moped. When his mother suggested, during an argument, that he was incapable of hanging on to money long enough because he couldn't stop buying drugs, he exploded in fury.

It is very important to let your teenager own his achievements without qualifying or undermining them, and similarly to let him face failure honestly without attempting to disguise or deny it. This is not the same as withdrawing your support or sympathy. Indeed, when things go badly your teen may need you to restate your faith in his ability, as his confidence may be at a low ebb.

7 Dare to let go

'Robert and I are a lot closer now,' reflected Julie Hunt. After a difficult period when Robert was helped to see the consequences of his actions, he began taking more responsibility for himself. He started showing an interest in his school work, and the intense focus on his gang activities was beginning to fade. 'I have to remind myself that he is a young adult who is responsible for his actions, whatever they may be,' Julie realized. 'I can't go on protecting him in that sense, only guide him.'

Handing back responsibility to your teenager for his own life while taking control of behaviour that impacts on your own is a difficult balance to achieve. For many parents, the idea of stepping back and letting their teenagers carry the can for their own choices feels very foreign. Although it may take time, if you are able to do it, most teens will eventually rise to the challenge.

For Sue Watts it was very hard to do, but she realized that she needed to show Suraj that she meant business in order to get more respect from him. The advantage was that once she started putting herself first, she began to feel less powerless. 'I can control my worries and my anxieties now,' Sue reflected.

While some responsibilities need to be given back to your teen, taking charge of your own life and protecting your own rights sends your teenager a further important message: he no longer needs to feel so responsible for you. You are affirming that you can look after yourself and that your happiness is no longer going to be solely determined by his actions. This can be an enormous release for both you and your teen. It can pave the way for a much more relaxed and comfortable relationship.

If you're finding it hard, it's worth remembering that at some point your teenager is going to leave home and will need to fend for himself. It is far better that he learns to take responsibility for himself in the protected environment of home before facing the less forgiving realities of life in the outside world.

POINTS TO REMEMBER
○ Strive for a balanced relationship with your teenager in which the needs of both teen and parent are recognized.
○ Remember that you have rights in this relationship too. Learn to stand up for them.
○ When tackling your teen's problem behaviour, try to identify how the problem affects her and how it affects you.

○ Try to focus your energies on the problems that affect you, while handing back responsibility for the problems that affect mainly your teen.

○ You can still express your feelings about the behaviour that affects your teen, but do so in a concise, structured way. Make it clear that you see it as his responsibility to deal with the problem.

○ Use home as a training ground to give your teen a head start for when he has to look after himself in later life.

chapter five

Boundaries and the bottom line

IN THE PREVIOUS CHAPTER WE SUGGESTED WAYS OF MAKING THE DISTINCTION between behaviour that affected your teen's life, and behaviour that affected your own. With the help of your diary you should now have a better sense of how and when difficult behaviour occurs, and when it's having an unacceptable impact on you.

Your teenager may appear to live in a world of his own much of the time, but if you or other family members are being directly affected by his behaviour, it's time to act. Whether you are smarting from your daughter's rudeness or simply fed up because your son makes you feel like an unpaid servant, it's a green light for action. Now is the time to think about putting some boundaries in place.

However much they grumble, most teenagers prefer to know where they stand. Your teenager needs reminding when her behaviour is unacceptable, and you need to make it clear that you will take decisive action to protect your rights and those of other family members. To reinforce this point you need to negotiate a system of clear rules backed up by effective consequences and sanctions if your teen cannot stick to them.

How to negotiate rules

'We stopped giving them money; they stole. We tried keeping them in; they jumped out of the windows. We've even got to the stage where we've stopped giving them birthday presents, and it just doesn't bother them,' complained Glynis Gibson of her 15-year-old twin sons Luke and Jonny. For Glynis and her husband Rob, finding the right system to discipline their sons seemed fraught with pitfalls. They felt as if they had tried everything.

On closer examination it turned out that what Glynis lacked was effective boundaries. She was allowing her sons to manipulate her with the promise of ever-worsening behaviour, and because she had no effective sanctions in place, they held her to ransom. But even if your teenager's behaviour is very bad, it should still be possible to come up with effective rules and sanctions. A key part of this involves thinking about what matters to your teenager and striving to create a system that will work for him.

Sometimes it's not so much the content of the rules as the way they are imposed that can have an impact on how they are observed by the teenager. After 22 years in the army, Ian Manson did not see rules as things that could be bent. 'The earlier you get used to the standing rules, the easier it is to stick to them,' he insisted. 'Everything has a line that you can't cross.' But this approach was anathema to his 16-year-old stepdaughter Jennie, who thought that getting home five or ten minutes late was no big deal.

Since Jennie and her stepdad were constantly fighting over rules, it was suggested that they try putting them to one side for a couple of weeks to break the endless cycle of arguing. Interestingly, Jennie responded by drawing up her own set of rules and doing more around the house without being asked to. More importantly, it meant that she was feeling much calmer about 'petty' rules when the time came to negotiate.

Drawing up your family contract

A helpful way of encouraging your teen to think about how his behaviour may be affecting others is to get him to participate in drafting a behaviour contract for the whole family. A well-designed family contract can prevent many potential problems developing, and provide a helpful reference point for dealing with future bad behaviour.

A family contract must not only outline the rules that various members are expected to follow, but should also make provision for clear consequences if the rules are broken. This way everyone knows where they stand. Everything should be written down and signed by each family member so there can be little argument about what has been agreed.

It is also important to establish the principles that provide the basis of your family rules. The Maddison Stokes family came up with three key principles: respect, responsibility and the importance of contributing to family life. These values became the reference point for the rules they agreed on. When 16-year-old Tom began behaving in an increasingly antisocial way, these principles helped to guide his parents' response.

Working with you on the contract will help your teenager to focus on the principles underlying your rules. Once she has acknowledged the justice of these principles for herself, and even played a part in deciding appropriate consequences when the rules are broken, she is much more likely to cooperate if and when those consequences have to be applied.

You need to be clear, however, that a family contract is supposed to be for the benefit of *everyone* in the family. Make sure that the phrasing is positive. If your teenager perceives this to be an ill-disguised attack on him, he will quickly rubbish your efforts. When David and Julie Hunt presented Robert with a contract that listed 'time management guidelines' and 'rules for handing in homework', Robert quickly deduced that these weren't family rules.

You might be thinking that as a well-behaved adult you actually don't need any rules for yourself. But you need to make sure that if you expect a certain standard of behaviour from your teenager, you are able to live up to it yourself. Timekeeping was a major issue with Robert, but he quickly took the opportunity to start attacking his mother Julie's own time management. This left stepfather David in a difficult position because he could see that Robert had a point. But by backing up his stepson against Julie, David gave the negotiation little chance of success. The Hunts' contract foundered before it had even got off the ground.

While you may be prepared for family members to identify aspects of your own behaviour that could change, don't forget whose house it is. This is not an opportunity for your teenager to have a go at you. However, if you do show willing, and perhaps even take on board a few minor restrictions yourself, such as not smoking in the house, or paying fines into a swear box, you will strengthen your own position when you need to discipline your teen.

Pick your battles

Sometimes teenagers can appear so out of control that it may seem like you need to overhaul every area of their behaviour to make an impression. But in fact you are unlikely to be successful if you attempt to tackle everything at once, and we would advise you not to try. It is far better to identify just one or two areas where you need to take a stand than to be over-ambitious and bite off more than you can chew.

Every case of bad behaviour you deal with effectively will increase your chances of future success. Your confidence and skill in managing your teenager will develop as you go along. Once your teen accepts your right to lay down a boundary in one area of his life, a precedent is established that should make it easier to extend your influence into other areas. You may also need to be pragmatic in choosing your targets: some of the behaviour that causes you the most heartache may not be the easiest or quickest to change. You need to identify the situations where you stand the best chance of making an impact.

As Glynis and Rob Gibson were struggling with their twin sons' behaviour at every level, they were asked to come up with a few key principles that they could stick to rather than trying to lay down the law in every area of their children's lives.

But they failed to do this. Instead they drew up a long list of house rules: no smoking in bedrooms, no loud music after 9.30 p.m., no friends allowed in the house overnight, no helping yourselves to money or cigarettes. They decided that if the boys broke the rules, everything would come out of their bedrooms but the beds. For the boys it was a call to battle. Unsurprisingly, when Glynis tried to present the rules to her sons she was greeted with volleys of abuse. She tried to put the rules into practice by removing Luke's music decks when he failed to get out of bed, and he responded by smashing up her dressing-table with a hammer. Glynis and Rob had tried to cover too much too soon, and it had provoked a lot of anger.

Involving your teen

When Jennie Manson sat down to negotiate with her mother and step-father, they focused on the two main areas of argument between them: what time Jennie came in, and the state of her bedroom. Although Ian believed that the best approach to coming in was to have a fixed time and stick to it, he was persuaded to agree a ten-minute 'buffer zone' after the coming-in time, which would not be counted as late. However, if Jennie then came in after the buffer zone, there would be a sanction: she would lose going out on a Friday or Saturday night.

In terms of the bedroom, Jennie agreed to make her bed, open her curtains, pick up washing and bring down dirty mugs. Her mother agreed not to nitpick about more general untidiness. The family agreed that Jennie could be given up to three reminders, and then a sanction would be imposed: one item, such as the television, would be removed from her room. Jennie and her parents each signed a copy, and it was pinned up where the whole family could see it.

Giving some of the control back to Jennie in negotiating the contract worked well for her. 'It's easier for everyone now there are set rules that all three of us have agreed to,' said Jennie. From then on she seemed to find it much easier to stick to her curfew.

Getting your teenager involved in negotiating the contract is key to its success. If he feels he has played a part in designing the contract and establishing its limits and consequences, he will own the process for himself and be much more likely to stick to it. This was exactly why Nia and John Pauley involved 15-year-old Dominic and 13-year-old James in discussing what rules they needed as a family, and what should happen if those rules were not obeyed. Below is an example of what they came up with.

SAMPLE FAMILY CONTRACT

What needs to be done	Consequences for not doing it
Laundry ● Put clean clothes away. ● Put dirty clothes in laundry basket. ● Dominic and James to get school clothes ready the night before.	● Clothes not in laundry basket won't be washed. ● Clothes left on floor – clean or dirty – will be bagged up and have to be bought back at 20p per item.
Bedrooms ● Floors to be kept clear of rubbish and clutter. ● Dirty mugs and plates to be taken downstairs and put in the dishwasher.	● If floor not clear for Friday evening inspection, all computer/internet access suspended until floor cleared. ● All computer access suspended until items put in dishwasher.
Computer and bedtime ● Dominic to be off the computer by 10 p.m. ● James in bed by 9 p.m. on school nights.	● If not off computer by 10 p.m., 15 minutes less computer time the following evening. ● If still up by 9 p.m., bedtime will be brought forward by 15 minutes the next night.

As well as agreeing to the consequences, Dominic and James were able to negotiate rewards for themselves if they stuck to the terms of the contract. If no clothes were collected in bin bags all week, no dirty mugs and plates were left around, and the bedroom floor was clear at Friday evening inspection, Dominic would earn internet access until midnight at the weekend, and James's weekend bedtime was pushed back by half an hour.

HOW TO NEGOTIATE

Part of your strategy for avoiding power struggles with your teen is to involve her as much as possible in negotiating the freedoms and privileges she wants. This will help her develop the skills she needs in learning how to get what she wants without resorting to tactics that may harm her or her relationships with others.

When negotiating with your teenager, try to keep the following principles in mind.

○ The goal of negotiation is to reach a win-win scenario, where everyone feels satisfied with the outcome. The goal is *not* to beat the other side into submission. You should look for solutions that will work for everyone.

○ Compromise may be needed to achieve your goal. You should cultivate a flexible, accommodating attitude, while remaining clear about the principles you will stand by and any concessions you are not prepared to make. This is your *bottom line*.

○ Think about what is motivating your teen's requests. Are there alternative ways of meeting the real underlying need that might be acceptable to both of you? For example, Jennie's 'buffer zone'.

○ Try not to take it personally if things get heated. It is important for you to set the tone by maintaining a rational position.

○ Finally, be aware that the negotiation is likely to go better if you have managed to build a relationship of trust and respect with your teenager. Ensure that you are taking the time and trouble to develop your bond with your teen away from the negotiating table.

Look out for loopholes

Your teenager might be happy to accuse you of petty nitpicking, but when it comes to bending the rules, she may well apply the letter of the law. When the Manson family drew up their behaviour contract with 16-year-old Jennie they forgot to say *how often* her room had to be tidied. As a result, Jennie later used this omission as an excuse not to do it. But even she found it hard to object when her mother presented her with the document she had signed agreeing that her parents could remove her TV after giving her three warnings. Before long the room was tidied.

Family meetings

A good way of keeping on top of how a family contract is working is to have a weekly family meeting. This is a regular get-together of no more than an hour when everyone can discuss any issues affecting family life, and grievances can be aired.

Every member of the family who is old enough should contribute to the meeting, perhaps by writing a topic on a centrally placed board, or putting ideas in a suggestion box. The meeting should have a chair-person, who will keep time and make sure that things run smoothly. Senior members of the family, including teenagers, can take it in turns to be the chair.

The meeting may be a good forum to assess whether weekly chores have been done adequately. The Maddison Stokes family planned their meeting for a Monday night to ensure that chores that had to be done by the previous Saturday lunchtime had been completed. They could then hand out Tom and Nick's weekly allowance. They also decided that they would use this opportunity to sit down and have a family meal, as it was rare for them all to be together.

But the Maddison Stokes family meetings often descended into arguments, particularly if the boys felt they were being criticized. That's why it's important to make sure that time is spent every week focusing on what has gone well rather than just concentrating on problems. The family meeting can be a great setting to give thanks and appreciation, acknowledge progress towards goals, and recognize that everyone in the family makes an important contribution.

If everyone is interrupting and talking across each other, it may help to introduce a 'talking spoon'. Only the person holding the spoon can speak, so everyone takes turns speaking and listening. Even a well-run family meeting may become fraught at times, so it can be a good idea to link it to a collective activity that everyone will enjoy afterwards, such as a take-away or a DVD.

If your teenager is in a rebellious frame of mind and doesn't want to play along with the meeting, it's best abandoned until he is feeling more cooperative. When Tom Maddison turned up to the family meeting very obviously stoned, Lesley made it clear that this was unacceptable and that he would not be getting his weekly money. Although he became verbally aggressive, she stood firm, so Tom got the message that there was a consequence for his behaviour.

The bottom line: setting consequences

If you have successfully drawn up a family contract and your teenager has agreed consequences with you, so much the better. However, sometimes you may have to impose consequences irrespective of whether your teenager agrees or not. In this case, you simply need to stick to your guns and plough on.

Sue Watts had got to the stage where she was fed up with being treated like a doormat. She and 16-year-old Suraj had negotiated an agreement between them where he would prove that he was responsible by texting her at 11 p.m. while he was out, to say that he was all right. He also agreed to cook a family meal once a week, and to stop smoking in his room. But when he went out he didn't bother to text, saying first that he had no credit and then that he 'forgot'. He not only continued smoking cigarettes in his room, but was smoking dope as well. As a result, he was stoned and made little effort when the time came to make the family meal. He also ran up a £264 phone bill, but refused to discuss it when his stepfather Phil tried to tackle him about it.

Sue and Phil decided that the time had come to impose sanctions on Suraj. Communication between them was at all-time low, so they decided to record a video letter informing Suraj of what they intended to do. Although Suraj was so enraged by this that he didn't watch it through, they had given him ample warning of what was to come.

Stick to your principles

Before you try to devise appropriate sanctions or consequences, it is vital to establish the basis upon which you are acting. While you should not have to justify yourself in all your dealings with your teen, it is important to recognize that the line 'Because I say so' is unlikely to cut much ice.

A child's ability in moral reasoning becomes more developed during adolescence, and your teenager should be able to take on board that there are principles behind your sanctions. For this to work you need to be clear about why you are insisting upon a particular standard of behaviour, and that you are not simply trying to control your teen's actions for the sake of it.

We have already suggested that your teen should be able to appreciate that other family members have rights too. Let your teenager know that when your rights are being violated you are entitled to protect them. He may need reminding whose house he lives in, who pays the bills and who provides the clean clothes, the lifts into town and other services. Don't be afraid to use these facts when encouraging your teen to respect you and your property.

You can also follow the principle that life in your household cannot be a one-way street. It is reasonable to expect your teen to do a few chores around the home, stick to the house rules and treat you and your partner politely. If he is unable to do this, then it is also reasonable to impose sanctions.

When you're thinking about appropriate sanctions, remember the principles behind them. If you concentrate on the importance of issues such as fairness, cooperation and respect, it may help you decide which behaviour you want to target and which you can afford to ignore.

Choosing the right consequences

Sue Watts decided that she would impose the following sanctions on Suraj: if he didn't pick up his clothes and put them in the laundry basket, they would go in bin bags; if he continued to smoke in his room, there would be no biscuits or treats to eat; and if she suspected him of smoking dope in his room, she would search it, confiscate any drugs she found and consider calling the police.

Suraj's response was that he 'didn't give a f***', but when he found himself with no snacks to eat at home, and all his clothes locked away in bin bags, he began to get the message. Although he insisted that his bedroom was private and Sue had no right to search it, Sue's response was entirely reasonable: 'Then don't do anything that's not legal,' she said. 'I don't want cannabis in the house. I won't search the room if there's no reason to.' She had made her position quite clear.

When it comes to choosing sanctions, they need to be tailored both to your teenager and to the particular behaviour. Different teenagers will rank the severity of particular consequences very differently. Teens who value their disposable income may be powerfully affected by a system of fines, whereas those whose main priority is freedom may be hit harder by an earlier curfew or a grounding. Restricting access to the use of the house phone or limiting time spent on the internet may have a dramatic impact on some teenagers, but leave others unfazed.

Spend a moment thinking about your own teenager and try to answer the following questions.

❍ What really matters to my teen?

❍ What does she like to spend time doing?

❍ What possessions or activities would he insist he could not survive without?

❍ Now think about the various services you provide for your teen and try to rate their importance to him as low, medium or high. Here are a few suggestions to get you started:

- Washing and ironing
- Shopping and cooking
- Pocket money/allowance
- New clothes/make-up, etc.
- Lifts and bus fares
- Internet access
- Use of the phone/mobile credit
- Access to TV
- Use of a room in your house as a personal space

- Opening your home to her friends
- Leisure activities – dance classes/sports events/cinema trips, etc.
- Enjoyable times together as a family

You can probably immediately identify a number of possessions or privileges that can be removed or suspended as sanctions for bad behaviour. However, you also need to make sure you pitch it right and choose the best consequence for the situation. If your teenager feels that your punishments are too harsh, he may dig his heels in.

If you start off too high up on the scale of sanctions, you will leave yourself nowhere to go should the situation escalate. Although you should aim to make the severity of the sanction reflect the seriousness of your teen's misbehaviour, it is better to put a slighter consequence in place and follow it through than it is to do nothing.

Effective consequences do not always involve taking something away. Depending on the situation, you could also ask your teenager to take on extra responsibilities or chores as a way of making amends.

The power of the pound

For many teenagers the most valuable currency is money. The chances are that even if they are doing some paid work, they are still dependent on you to fund their lifestyle. If you are holding the purse strings, you are in possession of an extremely effective bargaining tool, and this should not be underrated.

When the psychologists visited Luke and Jonny Gibson's bedrooms they were struck by the boys' material possessions: they had been given X Boxes, Game Cubes, PS2s... and all this in return for being excluded from school, smoking in their rooms and swearing at their mother. They also got a steady stream of cash no matter how they behaved.

Money for the boys equalled attention. Glynis giving them money however they behaved had an effect similar to giving a toddler a lollipop after he'd had a tantrum – namely, more of the same. So it was decided that Glynis and Rob should take a monetary approach to dealing with their twins' behaviour.

They were given a very simple system to follow, based on cash. Glynis decided that instead of the £50 she gave the boys in dribs and drabs every week, she would set them an allowance of £25 a week each, or £5 for each school day. To earn this they had simply to get up, get out of the house, get to school on time and pick up their clothes. Glynis kept a simple tick chart for every day; if they weren't out of the house on time or if they swore at her, they would lose their money.

Grounding – getting it right

For many teenagers there is no sanction that bites harder than being grounded. Most young people love getting out of the house, so being forced to stay in is punishment indeed. But while this sanction seemed to be the one most frequently applied among the families we met, it most often fails.

Lesley Maddison Stokes grounded her 15-year-old son Nick for two weeks, but when he was invited to a party during that period, she ended up chauffeuring him there and back. Similarly, Rob Gibson told his son Luke that he was grounded, but moments later allowed him to go out. Julie Hunt tried grounding Robert for two weeks, and she buckled too. 'Grounding doesn't work with Robert because he'll just have a big sulk, and he makes me feel bad,' she said.

In truth, if your teenager sulks about being grounded, it's probably the right consequence. Grounding *can* work, but it needs to be carefully thought through and consistently applied. One reason it often fails is that in the heat of the moment parents make it too big. 'You're grounded for two weeks' sounds like a really serious punishment. But 'You're grounded this Saturday' is likely to be much easier to put into effect.

HOW TO MAKE GROUNDING WORK

❍ Choose a specific time for grounding and ensure that you stick to it. If you decide that two weeks is the right amount of time, it needs to be two weeks. Remember, though, that shorter periods may be more realistic and easier to enforce.

❍ Define clearly what it means. It will be an ineffective punishment if you let your teen get in from school whenever he pleases, or hang around with friends outside the house in the evening.

❍ Don't give in, even if your teenager pleads that she has a special event to go to. Don't make any exceptions during grounding, except for school.

❍ If your teenager flaunts your grounding and goes out anyway, don't take this as your cue to give in. You need to apply another sanction, plus a sanction for breaking the grounding.

Think before you act

When you first start to lay down boundaries you may meet with some resistance, especially if your teenager is used to ruling the roost, so make sure you are able to clearly define the behaviour you need to target.

For example, it is no good announcing that you will no longer put up with 'rudeness' if you can't identify specifically what counts as rude behaviour. This might include:

❍ Not looking at me when I am talking to you.

❍ Calling me names.

❍ Ignoring me and walking away when I talk to you.

❍ Muttering under your breath.

❍ Answering me in a surly tone of voice.

Defining the behaviour in this way will help you to monitor it efficiently, make clear to your teenager what you expect, and make it easier for both sides to see when the rules are being broken.

If you have a partner, make the time to plan any sanctions together. It is important that you have agreed in advance what you are doing and why, as your teenager will drive a coach and horses through any inconsistency on your part. Make sure you back each other up in seeing it through. If you don't have a partner, consider talking your plans through with another parent or trusted friend, who may be able to spot things you have missed or make alternative suggestions.

Before you introduce sanctions you also need to ensure that you have thought through any possible drawbacks to your plans. This way your teenager won't catch you 'on the hop' with some loophole you may not have thought of. Try to anticipate any ways in which your teenager might attempt to thwart your sanction. Consider all possible contingencies.

For example, what will you do if your teenager refuses to be grounded and leaves the house without your permission? You could announce that the next time she leaves the home when she is grounded you will sell off a DVD or computer game (or clothes or shoes) from her collection for every thirty minutes she stays out. Or you could consider following her next time she goes out. The embarrassment of having a parent in tow may well do the trick.

Let the punishment fit the crime

Whenever possible, try to ensure that your sanctions follow on logically from your teen's actions. If your teenager refuses to help out around the house, you might consider not doing some of the domestic chores that make his life more comfortable.

Try to use an element of surprise in creating consequences. The impact of a humorous or dramatic response can sometimes get your message across more effectively. A pile of dirty dishes stacked carefully in your daughter's room with a label saying 'We belong in the dishwasher: can you help us find our way?' can be a good way of reminding her if she has failed to do her chores.

Darrel Patterson was asked to help move a dishwasher out of a new extension his parents were building to create a more spacious bedroom for him. Despite his parents' pleas, Darrel lay back on the sofa and refused point blank to help until they resorted to bribing him with money for his phone. They would have done far better to let Darrel take the consequences of his obstructive behaviour, either by leaving the dishwasher where it was in the middle of his new bedroom, or abandoning any further work on the room until Darrel was prepared to pull his weight.

If your teen damages your possessions, it makes sense that she should pay to replace them, either by sacrificing part of her allowance or taking on a part-time job to cover the cost of repairs.

If your teen has started breaking the law in a minor way, rather than shield him from the consequences of criminal behaviour, it might make more sense to involve the police yourself. Most parents are under-standably reluctant to do this, but, depending on the nature of the crime, many teenagers will get a caution for a first offence. However, the revelation that you will not protect him from the consequences of breaking the law may be enough to make your teen think twice before getting involved in other illegal activities.

When planning your response, also think about the underlying motives for difficult behaviour. Don't forget that if your teen's bad behaviour is really a means of acting out some inner conflict, you need to tackle the root of the problem, not just the symptoms. It's all right to respond to the behaviour with an appropriate sanction, but be aware that things are unlikely to change until the source of the underlying unhappiness is resolved.

Putting sanctions into practice

When the time comes to tell your teen about sanctions, make sure you get his attention, and identify the behaviour you are no longer prepared to tolerate. Give a *short* explanation of the way it affects you, and let your teen know what you intend to do the next time the behav-iour occurs. By doing so, you are giving him the opportunity to avoid the negative consequence. You should take the line that he is the one who has the power to determine what happens. Make sure you are

EFFECTIVE SANCTIONS NEED TO BE

Clear
- What are they for?
- How long will they last?

Appropriate
- Let the punishment fit the crime.
- Make it relevant to your teenager.
- Pitch it right.

Workable
- Think it through.
- Don't rush.
- Consider how you will monitor the behaviour and the sanction.
- Have a back-up plan.

clear about the terms of the consequences: what they will involve and how long they will last.

If your teenager refuses to listen, remain calm and simply carry out your plans. If your teen protests that you haven't given adequate warning, you can explain that you made an attempt to do so but he appeared uninterested in listening to you at the time. Follow through and next time around you will be guaranteed to have his full attention.

After limited success with paying their sons £5 a day to get out of bed and get to school on time, Glynis and Rob Gibson had to come up with more heavyweight sanctions. The urgency increased when Glynis discovered that Luke had used her credit card to buy records over the internet.

Together Glynis and Rob priced up everything in their sons' rooms: record decks £100, PS2 £75, PS2 games £10 each, TV £50. Now the boys were going to be fined: £10 every time they didn't go to school, £50 for stealing, and £1 every time they swore, argued or were disrespectful. They would still earn their basic £5 a day, but now they would have to do extra jobs around the house. If they lost more money in fines than they had actually earned, they would lose possessions for fixed periods.

Luke and Jonny looked stunned when their parents sat them down and gave them the new rules; but Luke was even more shocked when his parents announced an immediate sanction for stealing his mother's credit card. His precious record decks were going to be taken away for a week, and if he wouldn't accept it, his parents were going to the police. Luke raged and swore, walked out and came back again – but ultimately accepted the punishment.

That moment was a turning point for Luke. He even said he thought 'the rules were fair'. It was evidence that teenagers whose behaviour is out of control sometimes respond well to clear and reasonable boundaries. At least Luke knew where he stood.

However, his twin brother Jonny wasn't prepared to take the rules so seriously. 'She's said all that stuff before and it never happened,' he said of his mother. He was testing the system to see if it had any teeth. But Glynis stuck to her guns and kept applying the fines, and in time Jonny grudgingly accepted it. Three months later their parents reported that the twins no longer swore. 'They aren't as nasty as they used to be,' said Glynis, 'and we don't worry about money going missing.'

Be consistent

If you have said that you will act, it is crucial to do so. Unless you follow through, your teenager will correctly deduce that you do not really mean what you say. Whether your teen conjures up tears of remorse or flies into a rage, you must resist all attempts to manipulate you into going back on your word. You need to hold your ground and follow through with your planned consequence.

When Robert Kingdon stayed out all night, despite having a clearly agreed contract in place, his mother Julie had to follow through with the suggested consequences. As Robert had agreed to three nights' grounding for being more than 30 minutes late home, and had stayed out for an entire night, Julie clearly stated that he had broken the contract and for that he would be grounded for a week. Since the contract was already in place, Robert seemed unsurprised by the punishment, and more prepared to take it. 'You've got to give clear boundaries,' Julie realized. 'It's no good saying one thing and meaning another. You've got to stick by what you say.' For his part, Robert admitted that staying out all night 'wasn't worth it', suggesting that the grounding had made its mark.

The best part of a well-planned consequence is that it does the work for you. As a parent, you don't have to raise your voice or ask your teen to admit she is wrong. Once she has crossed your boundary, the time for talking and negotiating is over. You can accept an apology, but do not allow yourself to be swayed into giving in or giving up your sanction.

Start afresh

At one level a consequence is also an opportunity for your teen to pay for her misdeeds. Once she has 'done her time' and completed the punishment you've imposed, it is important that you both see the debt as cancelled and let bygones be bygones. You should allow your teenager a fresh start and try not to hold the past against her. Resist the temptation to embark upon a post-mortem or sneak in that final lecture.

This is the time when it is particularly important for you to pay attention to your teen's good behaviour and reinforce it with praise and appreciation. Remember, if you can create a positive environment where your children are encouraged when they behave in the way you want, you are unlikely to need many of the sanctions we have been talking about in this chapter.

The end of the road

We're not saying that effective discipline is easy, and there's no doubt that some teens are simply more difficult to discipline than others. Sometimes they get into situations where they find themselves in the grip of forces, such as drug use or peer pressure, that become more compelling for them than any sanctions you can impose.

But we are serious about the importance of defending your rights and protecting your personal well-being. It is ultimately down to the individual parent to determine what he or she is prepared to tolerate. However, if you feel your relationship with your teenager has become physically or emotionally abusive, you may have to consider whether you can afford to continue sharing your home with him.

Having made the call to Social Services to tell them that 16-year-old Tom was now homeless, Lesley Maddison Stokes was stunned. 'I can't believe that's where he's brought me to,' she reflected. But she knew that after Tom had smashed furniture in her home and been threatening and abusive about getting money that she had reached the end of the road. Although she was rightly very sad, she also felt that she had taken the best and only path available to her and husband Peter. She couldn't go on supporting Tom's behaviour by allowing him to live in her home.

Insisting that your teenager leaves home is a drastic step, and not one to be taken lightly or without proper consultation. But you may find that you have little option. If your teenager is violent towards you, repeatedly steals from you or is persistently threatening, you should not put up with it.

Sadly, people in all sorts of abusive relationships often become so exhausted that they lose faith in their power to change the situation. Do not let this happen to you. You have an ongoing responsibility not only to protect yourself and other family members, but also to your teen. If you stand firm, you will be giving your teen the clear message that there is certain behaviour that no one should have to tolerate.

Under such extreme circumstances, asking your teen to leave is simply to confront him with the consequences of his own actions. Emphasize that he has a choice, and make clear the conditions under which he can stay. However, if he won't agree to change his behaviour, you may have to follow through, however heartbreaking that decision.

Tom Maddison was eventually allowed back home after a spending a month in a city hostel and with friends. On his return, he wasn't making any promises, but his parents were adamant that he could only remain in the house on their terms. 'I wasn't going to make it easy for him to waltz back in here and pick up where he left off,' insisted Lesley. His stepfather Peter agreed: 'Tom knows we're not going to put up with anything that went on in the past – that's gone.'

You can do it!

If all this seems daunting, here are a few words of encouragement. Follow the principles in this chapter and most teens will respond in time. Don't expect any quick fixes, but make a resolution with yourself that, whatever happens, you won't give in and that you will start to take back control of your life. Your teen will test your resolve: that's part of her job. For your part, you need to make it clear that you will not be bullied or manipulated.

If you start to feel guilty or feel yourself weakening, just remember that the consequences you impose are the most effective way you can educate your teenager about the limits of acceptable behaviour and how her actions affect others. These are lessons that will not only make life at home better for everyone in the short term, but will also equip your teen to handle life in the outside world when the time comes for her to leave home.

POINTS TO REMEMBER

❍ Try to involve your teen as much as possible in negotiating rules and sanctions.

❍ Make it clear what your bottom line is, and don't allow your teenager to dissuade you from it.

❍ Choose your targets strategically – you don't have to address all the problems at once.

❍ Find consequences that are appropriate to the situation and to your particular teen.

○ Define the behaviour you are targeting in clear terms.

○ If you are applying a sanction, be clear why you are doing so.

○ Inform your teenager calmly that you are applying the sanction and why. Don't get angry or vengeful about it.

○ If your teenager is likely to object, make sure you think through your response carefully. Pitch it right and plan for every eventuality.

○ Always follow through and make your word count.

○ When your teen has accepted a consequence, wipe the slate clean and expect the best rather than the worst.

chapter six

Under pressure

MUCH OF OUR FOCUS SO FAR IN THIS BOOK HAS BEEN ON YOUR RELATIONSHIP with your teenager, and how his behaviour at home may be affecting you and your family. But many of the toughest issues you're likely to face may take place out of your sight. The teens are years when children start searching for kicks outside the home, and come under pressure to look and act in certain ways. They will have to deal with a range of influences, from school and friends to TV and magazines. They will also have to deal with the temptations of sex, drugs and alcohol. For parents, all this can be scary stuff.

Having a child who is going out drinking or skipping school might make you feel completely powerless as a parent. But if you can keep communication open with your teenager, and are able to negotiate clear boundaries that help her appreciate the advantages of more responsible behaviour, you will be better equipped than you think to deal with some of these tricky issues. While your teen may not actively seek your advice on sex or drugs, giving clear messages about where you stand on these issues is important in helping her to deal with them. As ever, while you cannot dictate how your teen behaves, you can offer support and make your position clear.

Peer pressure

'There's Rob the individual – nice lad, happy-go-lucky – and there's Rob in a crowd,' reflected David Hunt about his stepson. 'Whether he's easily led or just wanting to be seen as part of the group, it is affecting his school work.'

It's every parent's nightmare: your son or daughter is 'in with a bad lot' and you're worried that their behaviour is going downhill. Robert's gang was getting into fights and having brushes with the law; now a fight on school premises had led to his temporary exclusion. Robert insisted that he had been protecting some of his friends: 'It looks bad on me if my mates get hurt,' he protested.

For many teenagers like Robert, the recognition of their friends can be supremely important, and they'll go to any lengths to get and keep it. But while there's no doubt that the friends your teen selects can affect how he behaves, the way you react to these friendships can make all the difference.

Before you panic about the company your teenager is keeping, you need to ask yourself what the problem is. Are her friends really a 'bad lot'? Have you met them for yourself? Try not to jump to conclusions based on what you have heard or on what her friends are wearing. If your teen is dressing in a way you hate but coming in on time and keeping herself out of trouble, do the clothes matter so much?

Teenagers often feel insecure, and identifying themselves with a group or subculture can provide an instant identity that means they don't have to struggle with becoming themselves. You might find your teen's gang uniform unattractive, but it's not much different from the way we follow trends as adults; it's just that a work suit, designer buggy or a certain style of decorating your home may seem less controversial than a piercing or a tattoo. Thinking about some of the outfits you wore when you were younger may also help.

Sometimes joining a group of peers whose lifestyle is the opposite of everything you value or respect is your teen's way of achieving distance and longed-for independence from you. If you react strongly to the behaviour, clothing or slang that symbolize membership of your teen's chosen gang, she may be secretly delighted. Your horrified reaction is part of the pay-off. Despite knowing that her parents would explode when they found out she had pierced her own belly button, Gemma Taylor couldn't wait to let her mum Dawn 'discover' what she had done.

Don't always assume that the influence of peers is negative. You may find some surprising allies among your teen's friends. When 13-year-old Darrel Patterson was refusing to go home, even though he was already late, it was his mates who advised him to get going. When Suraj De and his friends came in drunk and noisy in the small hours, it was his friends who were caught on camera telling him how rude he was to his mum.

No place like home

Parents' concerns are often increased by the fact that they know so little about their teen's friends or what they do outside the house. Robert Kingdon's parents were horrified when they saw footage of what he was getting up to during an average night's troublemaking. But his mother Julie was also upset when Robert insisted that he'd rather be out with his mates than 'cooped up in the house'.

Teens who feel unwelcome at home quickly run out of places to hang around, and will often end up roaming the streets and getting themselves into trouble because there's simply nowhere else to go. One solution is to make it as easy as possible for your teen to invite his mates around. If you have the space, create an area in your home where he can entertain friends without disturbing you, but where you can still keep tabs on what's going on.

As Robert was sharing his bedroom with a much younger brother, he felt that he had nowhere in the house that was his own. His mother took him shopping and Robert chose some things to make his room feel more like his own space. Julie hoped that this would encourage him to stay at home more, and make it easier for him to invite friends back.

Ian Manson converted the bunker at the bottom of the garden for his 16-year-old stepdaughter Jennie, and installed a sofa, TV and play-station so that she could chill out there with her friends. Jennie was pleased with this, but when a fight broke out in the garden one night, her parents found their tolerance pushed to the limit. If your teen's friends behave in a way that you find unacceptable, you may need to withdraw your hospitality – it's still your house. But at least you will be basing your judgements on first-hand experience rather than relying on gossip or unfounded suspicions.

Many parents will have witnessed their teens instantly transforming themselves the minute their friends turn up at the door. However funny or annoying you find this, avoid humiliating your teen in front of his friends. He may never forgive you. If you need to tackle your teenager about his behaviour with his friends, it's best done when he is alone. Suraj De was furious when his mother reminded him in front of his friends to eat before going out drinking. She was concerned that he lined his stomach, but in his eyes this was a humiliation. 'It makes me look like I'm a little kid in front of my friends,' he protested.

The wrong crowd

If you've met some of your teen's friends, and feel that they *are* a bad influence, consider some of the following pointers. But tread carefully, as you may provoke your teen and make the situation worse.

1 'You don't even know them'

None of us likes it when other people criticize our friends, and your teen may be particularly prickly if you do so. Try to stick to the facts and avoid character assassination.

2 Set limits

Let your teen know that her friends are *her* business, but that you insist on firm limits relating to behaviour. If she doesn't respect those limits, you have a right to intervene. If she and her friends are behaving in a way that causes concern, contact her friends' parents and try to reach an agreement about how to handle the problem.

3 Share your own experience

Remind your teen that you were once a teenager yourself, and share any tough lessons of your own. When Julie Hunt revealed to Robert that her own unruly behaviour had landed her in Borstal, he saw her through new eyes.

4 Build self-esteem

After being helped to think more about his real values and what he wanted from his life, Robert Kingdon felt less compelled to go around causing trouble. Do everything you can to build up your teen's sense of self-worth. The more respect he has for himself, the less he will need to lean on the group, and the better he will handle peer pressure.

5 Don't cross-examine

Provide a listening ear if your teen does want to talk through issues she may be having with her friends. Try to help her solve her own problems and draw her own conclusions.

6 Keep talking

Look out for opportunities to talk with your teenager about the qualities you find in genuine friendships. How can you tell if someone has your best interests at heart? Would a real friend get you into trouble? Try to promote alternative friendships and activities that might reduce the negative influence of current friends.

7 Make home welcoming

Don't drive your teen into the arms of less desirable friends by creating an unfriendly atmosphere at home. Make time for your teen, and prioritize getting out and doing things together as a family. Emphasize that you are always there for her, no matter what.

Problems at school

Many of the teenagers we met on *Teen Angels* had problems with school. Some, such as Luke and Jonny Gibson and Gemma Taylor, had been excluded from mainstream school for disruptive behaviour. Others, such as James Ellis, were in trouble for not doing their work, while some, such as Anni Ellis, simply didn't turn up.

Since it's the place where your teenager spends most of his daytime hours, school is, of course, an enormous influence and possible source of stress. Not only does he have to deal with the pressures of studying, coursework and exams, but the social aspects of school life can also be a minefield for many teens. Any problems relating to school need handling with care.

Making the grade

Ian Manson and his 16-year-old stepdaughter Jennie were constantly arguing over her performance at school. 'I'm sick to death of bashing my head against a brick wall about you not bothering with your school work,' he shouted.

Like Ian, many parents spend a lot of time fretting about their children's success at school. What kind of job will she find? Will he get into college? But too much emphasis on exam results and homework can result in a good deal of stress and pressure. The brutal truth is that:

❍ You ultimately have very little control over whether your teen does her work in the way you would wish. However, you should make your expectations clear and you may wish to set up incentives to encourage good study habits.

❍ As a teenager, your child should be old enough to take responsibility for his own studies.

If you hang on to all the anxiety about your teenager's performance at school, you may prevent him from ever having to face that responsibility. Chris and Marie Ellis were naturally worried that 13-year-old James's failure to do his homework properly was going to have an impact on his future. But in James's case the best way forward was to let him take responsibility for his work himself.

Other teens may need more active support with their studies, even if they are too proud to ask for it. Stepfather Tim Hull set aside time to help 13-year-old Darrel Patterson with his homework, and it was clear that his input made a real difference. Your aim should be to build your teen's confidence and encourage him without taking over. Try talking with your teen about what he might find useful, and discuss the role he would prefer you to play. If he is struggling with particular subjects, ask his permission to liaise with the school for advice on strategies that might help.

What's going on?

If your teenager starts having problems at school, try thinking as broadly as you can about any problems that might be making it hard for her to apply herself. Teens who are depressed will find it hard to concentrate or feel motivated. Remember that your priorities may be different: while you're worrying about her grades, she might be more concerned about bitchy remarks in the dinner queue, or what will happen if she goes out with her best friend's boyfriend.

Sometimes peer pressure can be having a negative effect. Although academically able, Gemma Taylor was worried about what her mates would think if she buckled down at school. Faced with the choice of being seen as 'sound' or a 'gimp', she preferred to go on being disruptive; before long she was excluded from mainstream education.

Some teens who become disruptive may be frustrated by their inability to keep up in class. Unruly behaviour can distract attention from learning problems, or even get them excluded at a time when they really need support. Before you assume that your child is simply unmotivated make sure that he is not genuinely struggling with his studies. Learning difficulties often become apparent during the teenage years, so if you do feel that he has unrecognized problems, talk to the school about arranging for assessments.

Bullying

Thirteen-year-old James Pauley was constantly getting into fights at school, partly because he was being picked on. If your teen tells you he is being bullied, pay close attention. First, let him know that he doesn't have to suffer in silence and that he has done the right thing in coming to you. Point out that bullies are always trying to get a reaction, and that, when possible, he should ignore them and seek out the company of his friends. It is generally not a good idea to advise your teen to retaliate: he may get hurt, or end up being the one who gets into trouble.

Bullies tend to pick on people who appear isolated or vulnerable, so teach your teenager to walk tall and project a sense of confidence, whatever she may be feeling inside. Check out the school's anti-bullying policy and be prepared to talk to staff if necessary, but always discuss things with your teen before you take any action. Get her to keep a log of any bullying incidents and to save any text messages or other evidence of what is going on.

Bunking off

Marie Ellis knew that her daughter Anni had skipped school at times during the previous year, but she thought that was all in the past. So when the school phoned to say that Anni had not been in on several occasions, Marie was devastated.

School attendance is one area where you definitely have to get involved. You have a legal obligation as a parent to make sure your child attends school until the age of 16. So if your teen is bunking off, it's not just a problem that will affect his life, but yours as well. Make this very clear to your teen, but try to find out why he is truanting. Is he being bullied? Is he struggling with the work? Is something else going on in his life that you don't know about?

Getting to the root of Anni's truanting proved difficult. Initially she denied it, and persuaded her mother that she had been in school all along. But Anni's parents were still suspicious, and when her father caught her back at home an hour after she had officially left for school, they thought the worst.

In a session with a psychologist Anni admitted to her parents that she had missed some lessons. But she revealed that she had felt unable to talk to them about it, as the last time she had missed school was during her mother's treatment for skin cancer. 'Everyone was concentrating on my mum,' Anni recalled. 'It sounds really selfish, but I couldn't cope. I thought the only option was that I just won't go, I won't have to see my teachers, I won't have to let it be dealt with.'

Anni's parents happily agreed that they would give her more support if she needed it. But when the school phoned again and revealed that Anni's attendance was down to 61 per cent, they lost patience and gave her an ultimatum: go to school or leave and get a job.

Anni finally confessed that she was having problems coping with the workload. 'Before it was easy to do well at school, and now it's not coming naturally,' she admitted. Feeling that she could barely cope, she had panicked and stopped attending. By finally owning up to all the problems she was having, Anni turned the corner. She had to have a slip signed at the end of every lesson to say that she had been there, and she started seeing a counsellor about future coping strategies.

Absenteeism can become a seductive habit for many teens. The more school they miss, the harder it becomes to catch up, and the less they can face going. For this reason it's important to take the initiative before your teen gets into the habit of missing school. For a few teens school refusal is rooted in psychological problems, such as fear of leaving home, or a genuine phobia. These types of problem require specialist professional help. However, such cases are rare, and for the majority truanting is usually about avoiding something specific.

What to do about bunking off

Whatever the reason your teen is missing school, make it clear that you will help him work through any problems, but that staying off is not an option. Make a contract with him and, if necessary, create some kind of incentive scheme to reward improved attendance.

You can try to explore practical reasons for going to school that will make sense to your child, such as thinking about the kind of job she might want and how school might help her get there. Be aware, though, that many teenagers are rooted in the present, and the future can seem too remote to worry about.

It's also important to develop a working alliance with the school. Go in and talk to staff about how you can keep your child in school.

Remember that your child's presence at morning registration does not mean she will still be there at lunchtime. If you are out at work, organize a system where you can ring to check your teen's whereabouts at strategic points in the day. Cooperate with any system that the school puts in place, such as signing report cards.

The odds of your teenager staying in school are greatly improved if he can get there in the first place. Darrel Patterson's parents had to set off for work very early, before Darrel was out of bed. This meant that Darrel sometimes simply wouldn't bother going to school. If you have to leave the house before your teenager, you need to find a system for ensuring that he gets up and leaves the house, or the chances are he won't make it. Try to find someone who can make sure that your teen gets to school, or use your school's breakfast club, if there is one. You may have some hard choices to face. Can you modify your hours to allow you to be there at the beginning of the day? Would a change of job allow more flexibility? You may have to accept that sorting out the problem will mean some short-term inconvenience for you.

Body image and eating problems

'I just made myself sick. I feel horrible. I don't even know why I've done it. I feel fat and ugly and everything's getting me down.' Fifteen-year-old Elane Parkinson's tearful confession to her video diary was a painful reminder of how quickly some distressed teenagers can translate their unhappiness into attacks on themselves and their bodies.

As it turned out, Elane wasn't suffering from a serious eating disorder, but, like many teens, she used food-related behaviour as a way of dealing with troubled emotions. On this occasion she had argued with friends and felt overwhelmed with emotion. She made herself sick as a way of feeling better, although it hadn't proved a good way of coping.

Over 6 feet tall and very slim, Elane had hopes of becoming a model, and was constantly reminding herself to 'think skinny'. Nevertheless, she confessed that when she looked in the mirror she still saw a 'fat, horrible person'. She was therefore at risk of feeling vulnerable whenever she put on so much as a pound. Elane's 17-year-old sister Lucie shared the sentiment that when she too looked in the mirror she also saw a 'big, horrible, ugly, fat person'.

Elane and Lucie needed help to understand that their happiness need not be dependent on the way they looked, and that their relationship with food was affecting the way they felt about themselves. They would often binge eat on fattening snacks, such as Yorkshire puddings, and Lucie ate up to seven packets of crisps a day. Then they would miss meals to compensate for the bingeing, which would make it more likely that they would eat more later on.

Many teenagers are acutely sensitive about their appearance, and this is hardly surprising when so much of teenage culture implies that only particular sizes and shapes are attractive and desirable. Our image-obsessed culture screams at us that only supermodel-thin equals good, and this leaves many teenagers feeling under-confident and demoralized. Teenagers with a weight problem are often the butt of cruel jokes and can struggle to feel accepted among their peer group. So it's important to be able to recognize when an eating disorder may be setting in.

It's no coincidence that when the Taylor family was asked to write down a list of banned terms that no one in the family was to use when speaking to each other, all of Gemma's were names such as 'fatty' and 'whale'. It is really important to clamp down on this kind of name-calling because it can have a profound effect on even a robust teen's self-image.

Recognizing an eating disorder

The two most commonly recognized types of eating disorder are anorexia and bulimia. Anorexia usually involves a terror of gaining weight or becoming fat, even though the sufferer may already be very underweight. A bulimic will suffer from recurrent episodes of out-of-control binge eating followed by drastic attempts to prevent weight gain through self-induced vomiting, periods of fasting, or excessive bouts of exercise or use of laxatives. It is possible for the two conditions to coexist, and someone with anorexia may also demonstrate bulimic behaviour. Although eating disorders affect mostly females, some male teens suffer from these problems too.

Some teens' eating becomes disordered simply because they are trying to make themselves more acceptable to their peers and themselves. For others weight seems to be the one thing they feel they can control, and regulating it becomes a dangerous obsession. There are nearly always underlying anxieties and issues about self-worth behind most eating disorders. Restricting food can be a self-inflicted punishment for a perceived inadequacy, just as over-eating can be a way of self-soothing or escape. Like any drug, these techniques can become powerfully addictive.

Eating disorders are usually secretive affairs, and sufferers often become highly skilled at covering their tracks. However, watch out for the following signs:

○ Dramatic weight loss or gain – although your teen can still remain the same weight while having an eating disorder.

○ Wearing baggy clothing to disguise her figure.

○ A preoccupation with weight and the calorie content of foods.

○ Frequent trips to the bathroom, especially after meals. Some bulimics will leave the tap running to hide the noise of vomiting.

○ Hiding food around the house.

○ Compulsive exercising.

○ Reluctance to eat in the company of others.

○ Discovery of diet pills or laxatives in your teen's room.

○ Bizarre food rituals or vague patterns of eating.

○ Mood swings.

○ Preoccupation with diet books and food diaries.

○ Other physical signs, such as hair loss, or increased hair growth on face and limbs, a pale complexion, dizziness, frequent headaches, missed periods, joint pain and constant sore throats.

IF YOU SUSPECT AN EATING DISORDER...

Take it seriously, even if you think your teenager is just attention-seeking or trying to alarm you. Eating disorders can be very hard to deal with once they become established, and can cause significant health problems, or even prove fatal. Most teenage girls experiment with diets from time to time, but if you suspect a more serious problem, seek a referral to an eating disorder service.

Don't focus just on eating. Remember that eating disorders are a coping strategy for dealing with distress. At the root of most eating difficulties is usually very poor self-image. Try to be open to these under-lying problems by adopting a gentle, sympathetic approach no matter how anxious your teen's behaviour may be making you. Encourage her to identify her feelings, and problem-solve with her to find alternative ways of coping with them.

Keep serving meals. Do continue to provide healthy, regular meals, preferably eaten at the table together as a family. Try to keep the topic of conversation away from weight or eating. Remember that you cannot force your teen to eat, and if you try, you might make her even more determined to resist you.

Inform your teenager. Make sure your teen has access to relevant information. Elane Parkinson was surprised to learn that cycles of restricting food and binge-eating confuse the body, making it more likely that fat supplies will be laid down rather than reduced. Many teens whose eating is disordered do not appreciate the risks they are taking with their health. (See page 147 for further information.)

Encourage self-worth. Do everything you can to help your teen feel good about himself and his body. Challenge damaging assumptions that physical attractiveness and happiness are the same thing, or that looks are the most important aspect of a person.

Hot to trot: your teen and sex

As bodies mature and hormones surge, the topic of sex is going to be high on your teen's agenda, regardless of whether or not he is sexually active. The teens who took part in *Teen Angels* were no exception. Several were involved in relationships, but for reasons of privacy we won't supply details.

Facing the facts

We live in a society that exerts intense social and cultural pressures around sex. Media images constantly link sexual attractiveness to personal worth, so it's hardly surprising that many teens come to view an active sex life as proof of their adult status. Sex allows teens to develop a new sense of their identity, and can satisfy universal teenage cravings for closeness, acceptance and stimulation.

Seeing your precious baby wearing a T-shirt proclaiming him to be a 'Mean Lean Love Machine' might come as a shock, but the reality is that just under 20 per cent of girls and just under 30 per cent of boys will have had sexual intercourse before they reach the age of 16. Although this means that the majority are still *not* having full sex by this age, if you're parenting a teenager, sex is clearly a topic that you cannot afford to ignore.

Research has also found that teens in families that have been through divorce or separation are more likely to be sexually active at a younger age than others. The precise reason for this is not known.

Your role

With so much media discussion about sex, and sex education being offered in schools, it might be easy to assume that your teenager will know it all. In reality many teenagers have rather a sketchy knowledge of some of the facts. A recent study discovered that some teens knew more about HIV than they did about the basic facts of fertility.

Peers are not always the most reliable sources of information either. Misinformation gets passed around and peer pressure can mean that your teen is given the misleading impression that 'everyone else' is doing it and that she will be 'left out' or made fun of if she doesn't join in.

That's why it's so important to talk to your teenager about sex. Your role is to help your teenager see the importance of valuing herself, not feeling pressured into having sex before she feels ready, and respecting others in sexual relationships. It's also more likely that if your teen has a strong sense of self-worth, she will only go ahead with sex when she feels ready, and is more likely to take personal safety seriously.

Many teens feel uncomfortable talking about sex with their parents, but don't let this put you off. The most important thing you can do is to cultivate a relationship in which your teen is able to talk to you when he needs to – whatever the subject. As your teenager enters the choppy waters of relationships and dating, it's important that you show him you can talk about sex without being judgemental. The more you can show that you understand it's a healthy and exciting part of growing up, the better.

If you really can't face talking about sex, try at least to point your teenager in the direction of websites or helplines that may be useful (see page 147).

Not just birds and bees

It is crucial that teens of both sexes understand the risks of unwanted pregnancy and sexually transmitted diseases, and know how to protect themselves against them. Many teens still do not appreciate that the only way they can adequately protect themselves against sexually transmitted diseases, such as chlamydia and HIV, is by using a condom. Similarly, many teenage pregnancies occur because teenagers feel embarrassed buying condoms, or don't know how to use them properly. If you suspect your teenager is sexually active, or even considering becoming so, you should make sure he has access to condoms or supply them yourself.

Buying condoms for your son or daughter is not the same thing as encouraging them to have sex, and you can make this distinction very clear. You're showing that you're concerned for your teen's well-being. Of course you should sensitively let your teen know if you think she may not be ready for sex. But if the reality is that she is going to have sex, you can help make sure it's safe.

Good sex education also means helping your teenager develop the skills to deal with the situations in which he may find himself. Sex is more likely to happen in situations where alcohol is involved, or where there is little adult supervision. Helping your teen to understand the effects of alcohol on his sexual behaviour may also be a good idea.

Underage sex and the law

Although many teenagers are sexually active under the age of 16, the legal age of consent for sex between a male and a female or between two males is still 16. There is no age of consent for sex between two females. Sexual contact of any kind with a minor is an offence. Your son needs to know that if he has sex with a girl under 16, he could be charged with statutory rape; if your daughter is under 16, she should understand that her partner could be prosecuted. If your son gets a girl of any age pregnant, he could be responsible for supporting that child as it grows up.

Although prosecutions between teenage partners of similar ages are relatively rare, you need to protect your child's well-being. If you do have concerns about a sexual relationship that your underage son or daughter is having, you should contact your GP or Social Services who will be able to advise you.

Always be alert to situations where there is clearly an imbalance of power, such as teenagers having sex with someone older than themselves, or a situation in which you feel there might be exploitation or pressure to have sex.

Dangerous escapes

Teens who are keen to escape confused or painful mood states, or simplythe boredom of daily life, may be tempted by a range of mind-altering substances easily available to them. Alcohol is commonplace, but it may surprise you to learn how little effort it would take your teen to lay her hands on a number of other substances, ranging from ecstasy to heroin and cocaine. Dealers know that teenagers are easy targets, and peer pressure to take drugs socially can be intense. Many teens will end up trying the fashionable drug of the moment simply to avoid being labelled as uncool or cowardly by their friends.

While the short-term effects of some drugs can be highly pleasurable, no drug is risk-free, and some can have significant consequences for your child's physical and mental health. It might be easy to bury your head in the sand when confronted with a world that feels alien to you, but you need to pay attention if you suspect your teenager is using drugs of any kind.

Teenagers and alcohol

Fifteen-year-old Rob Kingdon's face was the picture of innocence when his mother Julie asked him if he'd been drinking. He gave a spirited denial, but couldn't keep it up when Julie saw footage of him swigging vodka out of a coke bottle down at the recreation ground. The truth was that every Friday and Saturday night he and his friends drank as much as they could lay their hands on.

Alcohol remains the most widely used mood-altering substance used by teenagers. Although teens cannot technically buy alcohol until they are 18 (except with a meal), research shows that by the age of 15 some 45 per cent of boys and 35 per cent of girls are drinking on a weekly basis, and a third of 15-year-olds claim to drink alcohol in a bar at least once a week. The truth is that alcohol is readily available, and your teen is going to be offered plenty of opportunities to drink it.

Teenagers drink for various reasons, many of which they share with adult drinkers. Alcohol can relax you and boost social confidence. It can offer temporary relief from feelings of boredom or stress. For many teens drinking is a way of acting grown up, while others drink because their friends are doing it and they want to feel part of the in-crowd.

It's very unlikely that you will be able to stop your teenager from drinking if he wants to. But it's important he understands that although alcohol may make him feel more confident, it may also make him more vulnerable. As teens often have less physical bulk than fully grown adults, even modest amounts of alcohol can have a potent effect on them, particularly when they lack the confidence or control to say no to another drink.

Given all these factors, you should prepare your teen to make sensible choices about alcohol, and make him aware of some of the risks of drinking:

○ Drinking removes inhibitions. (Your teen is far more likely to get into fights, commit crimes or have unwanted sex under the influence of alcohol.)

○ Binge drinking can cause alcohol poisoning, leading to coma, or even death.

○ Tolerance to alcohol increases over time, meaning you may need to drink more to achieve the same effect.

○ Long-term heavy drinking can lead to a number of health problems, including liver damage, stomach cancer and heart disease.

If you yourself drink, you can set your teenager an example by showing how alcohol can be consumed in modest quantities. You may want to encourage a sensible attitude to drinking by letting your teenager try small quantities of beer or wine at home, but this needs to be done consistently, as your teenager may look for loopholes. Fifteen-year-old Dominic Pauley was allowed to drink one beer at home at the week-ends. But when his father started allowing him to drink beer on week nights, his mother didn't like it. Dominic started helping himself to beers without asking when his father was out, which caused tension between him and his mother. He also tried to exploit his father's agreement to his having some beers to take to a party by getting hold of an entire crate of beer and hiding it in the garden shed.

Remember, you may reluctantly accept that your teen is going to drink, but you should not have to put up with the unpleasant consequences of his choices. Sue Watts was unhappy about her son Suraj returning home drunk with his friends and waking her up in the small hours. Suraj's stepfather Phil was particularly angry about several occasions when he had had to clear up vomit after Suraj had been out drinking. If your drunken teen throws up, don't clean up after him, but wake him up bright and early the next morning with a bucket and mop, or present him with the bill for having the carpet cleaned.

TIPS FOR TEENS BEFORE DRINKING

Encourage your child to take the following steps in order to cope with alcohol and its effects.

❍ Have something to eat before drinking so that alcohol gets into the bloodstream more slowly.

❍ Always drink in the company of people you can trust, and make sure you have made plans for getting home safely.

❍ Try to alternate alcoholic drinks with soft ones.

❍ Spirits are much stronger than wine or beer, and even sweet-tasting drinks, such as alcopops, contain as much alcohol as beer.

❍ Be careful when mixing drinks. Consuming alcohol of different strengths, i.e. beer, wine and spirits together, can make it harder to keep track of the number of units consumed and may increase drunkenness.

❍ Do not leave drinks unattended when drinking in public places, and make sure you have seen the drink being poured.

Teenagers and drugs

Lesley Maddison Stokes was desperately worried about 16-year-old Tom. When she saw footage of him smoking 'bongs' she wasn't surprised. 'I knew it was coming,' she said, but she had no idea how to deal with it. Although Tom spoke of wanting to stop smoking dope, he seemed to be locked in a cycle of smoking it every day. Eventually he admitted that he couldn't stop thinking about dope, and was finding it extremely hard even to cut down.

Although alcohol remains the most popular drug, most teenagers will probably come into contact with a wide array of other mood-altering substances, which could include ecstasy, cocaine and heroin. Cannabis, or dope, in particular is widely used by teenagers. At the end of the 1990s it was estimated that 40 per cent of 14- to 16-year-olds in the UK had smoked it at least once.

There has been much recent debate in the press about the safety of cannabis. Although it is mostly considered to be a fairly harmless drug, some studies suggest that cannabis may have a harmful effect on brain development in younger teens. There is also a chance that for some teens cannabis can act as a gateway to harder drugs. Remember, too, that marijuana smoke contains 50–70 per cent more carcinogenic hydrocarbons than tobacco smoke, as well as an enzyme that might increase the risk of developing cancer.

Although cannabis is not physically addictive in the way that heroin or cocaine can be, a small percentage of users do develop a psychological dependence on the drug, as Tom Maddison discovered when he tried to stop smoking. Side-effects for heavy smokers of cannabis can include:

❍ Feelings of paranoia, anxiety and fretfulness.

❍ Problems with coordination and concentration – particularly dangerous if your teen is driving.

❍ Loss of short-term memory.

❍ Various health risks associated with smoking, including heart problems, bronchitis and cancer.

❍ Loss of motivation.

❍ Possible mental health problems, such as psychosis, in those with a predisposition towards them.

Dealing with drugs

Some level of experimentation with 'soft drugs', such as alcohol, tobacco and cannabis, should probably be regarded as normal teenage behaviour. But although there is little you can do to stop your teen experimenting with drugs when out of the house, this doesn't necessarily mean you have to approve. As with alcohol, you need to ensure that your teenager understands the risks associated with drugs, and set clear boundaries around what happens in your home.

If you don't want drugs brought into the house, you can make this clear by reminding your teen that he is causing you to commit an offence if illegal drugs are knowingly consumed on your premises. Sue Watts told her son Suraj that she would search his room if she thought he was smoking dope in the house, and Lesley Maddison Stokes threat-ened to call the police when Tom and his friends gathered to smoke in the garage.

If you suspect your teenager may be developing a drug problem of any kind, keep a close eye on the situation because she may need your help. There will inevitably be a number of telltale signs, even if your teen swears blind that nothing is wrong and that she has the situation under control.

SIGNS OF POSSIBLE DRUG USE

○ Abrupt mood changes, unexplained lack of motivation, increased levels of restlessness and irritability, or dramatic changes in sleeping patterns – although do not rule out other explanations.

○ If your child suddenly always needs money or items of value go missing.

○ If your teen suddenly stops mixing with his old friends and seems reluctant to tell you much about the people he now hangs out with.

○ You can often detect the smell of alcohol, tobacco or marijuana on your teen's breath. Smoking dope may give your teenager red eyes and a desire to eat (known as the 'munchies'), and he may appear giggly or sleepy.

○ Heavy alcohol use can lead to a flushed appearance, dilated pupils, clumsiness and difficulty focusing.

○ Amphetamines or cocaine can make the user extremely animated, erratic and sometimes agitated. Long-term use of cocaine may lead to unexplained nosebleeds.

○ Pinpoint pupils, scratching and constant nodding off suggest heroin use. Long clothing may be used to disguise injection marks, and look out for burns on lips or fingers.

What can parents do?

It can be a shock to discover that your teenager is using drugs, and you may feel angry or frightened. But it's important to take a step back and think about how you are going to deal with the situation. While you can't actually stop your teenager from taking drugs, having a coping strategy may help you feel less powerless.

1 Keep calm

If you think your teenager is taking drugs, it's important not to panic. If you overreact, you could make the situation worse. Although you may feel shocked about it, try to remember that teenagers often use drugs to escape underlying feelings of despair or self-hatred. Your teen may need to confront these issues before she can deal with the drug use.

2 Get informed

You'll need to have the facts at your fingertips if you're going to have any useful discussion with your teen about his drug use. If he thinks you don't know what you are talking about, he will switch off. (See page 147 for sources of further information.)

3 Get talking

Talk to your teen about your concerns, but avoid being confrontational or judgemental. You can't make her stop using drugs, but it is important to try to help her find her own motivation to change. Try to focus on behaviour you have witnessed, and explain why it has troubled you. Emphasize that you want to understand and help in any way you can. If your teen becomes abusive or angry, keep calm and bring the conversation to a halt. Tom Maddison smashed a table in fury when his parents were trying to talk to him about his drug use. This was their cue to end the conversation.

4 Get help

If your teen acknowledges that he has a problem, encourage him to seek professional help. Any attempt to reduce drug use will stand a better chance with support from a trained drugs counsellor, but it may be difficult to get him to this point, particularly if he is denying the severity of the problem. Suraj De became angry and abusive when his mother suggested he see a drugs counselling service. Your GP will be able to advise you about local services, or you can search the drugs websites (see page 147).

5 Set limits

Tom Maddison was beginning to frighten his parents with threatening behaviour. Suraj De began stealing from his mother's purse. If your teenager begins to cause problems in the home as a result of drug use, you need to point out calmly that you cannot put up with such behaviour indefinitely. You may need to make it a condition of continuing to live in your house that your teen behaves more reasonably, or gets involved in a suitable treatment programme. If you give your teenager an allowance, you can also ensure that it is strictly controlled, or even stopped if the money is going on drugs.

6 Encourage alternatives

Although you may be feeling helpless, it's important not to give up on positive solutions. Try to encourage activities and friendships that are non-drug related. It will help to give your teenager focus if you can put something else into his life that might build his confidence and sense of self-worth.

7 Don't go it alone

Many parents feel unnecessary shame about their child using drugs, and tend to keep it to themselves. But handling a situation like this can be highly stressful, and you will need all the support you can get. Involve other family members, friends or other parents as your teen may find it harder to dismiss people outside the immediate family group as interfering and over-anxious. Addictions flourish in secrecy, so the more you can flush them out into the light of day, the harder it will be for your teen to keep running from the problem.

8 Be prepared to let go

If, after you have tried everything you can do to help, your teenager continues to use drugs, you may decide that your best course of action is to let go of the problem and leave it to her to sort out. However painful it is for you, the only person who can stop taking drugs is the teenager herself.

The truth is that some teens won't find the motivation to change until they start experiencing the reality of what drugs can do to their lives. For some people the quicker they hit rock bottom, the sooner they will start to sort out their life. By trying to protect your teen indefinitely from the consequences of her bad choices, you may actually be prolonging her relationship with drugs and even allowing a more severe addiction to take hold. However, if you are facing hard choices like this, make sure you talk to an appropriate professional first. There are several good organizations that offer support and guidance for parents (see page 147).

chapter seven

Teen building

IN THE PREVIOUS CHAPTER WE SUGGESTED THAT THE TEENAGERS MOST ABLE TO resist peer pressure and steer clear of drug-taking and crime are those with a healthy sense of self-esteem. If your teenager feels good about himself, you have a much better chance of keeping him out of trouble, and happy too. And as you no doubt already know, a happy teen is a lot easier to live with than a miserable one.

People often misunderstand what is meant by self-esteem. It doesn't mean being self-obsessed, or acting like you're 'God's gift': in fact, such behaviour is often an attempt to cover up underlying feelings of inadequacy. True self-esteem means both valuing yourself as a worthwhile person and knowing that you deserve to be treated with respect by others.

But feeling good about oneself as a teenager can be a tall order. During the teenage years self-esteem is constantly under attack. This is the time when your child can be most vulnerable to self-doubt and negative inner voices. She also needs to work out who she is, where she is headed and what she stands for. You can play a vital role in helping your teenager to feel good about herself and develop skills for handling her feelings as she finds her way.

Developing your teenager's self-esteem can prove a worthwhile investment. It may protect him and you from the poor behaviour and personal problems that affect many people with low self-worth. So spend a few moments thinking about some practical ways in which you can instil greater self-belief in your teen. Use your diary to monitor his behaviour as you put your strategies into practice, and see for yourself whether they are making a difference.

Work at your relationship

As he's growing up, a young child's self-image depends almost entirely on the kind of interaction he has with those who care for him. Although other people begin to have more influence on this during the teenage years, one of the best ways you can nurture your teenager's sense of self-esteem is through your relationship with him.

Your teen depends on you for positive feedback, so let him know that he is doing all right. If you are constantly critical or dismissive of what he does, he's going to grow up with a sense of not being good enough. It's important you help him build his sense of self-worth by finding ways to demonstrate your love and support. Make a special effort to give positive feedback about things that please you.

You can't assume that your teenager will automatically know that you love her. Helen Ryan had become convinced that the only way she could show her love for her two demanding teenage daughters was through spending money on them. She was asked to find ways of showing her girls that she cared about them which didn't cost anything. When she sat down and told Lucie and Elane that they were 'much cleverer and more talented than they think they are, and should be proud of themselves' it was a breakthrough moment. The girls were delighted. 'It's stuff we've never heard about each other,' said Lucie. 'I've got butterflies in my stomach!' Moments later mother and daughters were able to hug for the first time in ages. Helen also started going along to watch Lucie at her Irish dancing classes, and taking pleasure in her achievements. It's important to make the time to support your teenagers' achievements and delight in their success. Equally, if they manage to cope with tricky tasks or situations, notice it and compliment them.

Making time just to 'hang out' with your teen also sends an important message to him about how much you value your relationship.

Finding activities that you both enjoy, or even taking up a new interest together, can help bring you closer and develop your teen's confidence. After a lot of fighting and friction, Ian and Jennie Manson were asked to cook Sunday lunch together. It was a perfect opportunity for Ian to encourage Jennie in something she did well, and to help build her sense of competence.

Tim and Kim Hull had a hectic schedule that involved getting up for work at 5 a.m. every day. When they returned home, 13-year-old Darrel would go out with his mates. By the time he got in, his parents were ready to go to bed. Although they were tired, Tim and Kim were asked to stay up an hour later so they could make themselves available to Darrel between 9 and 10 p.m. each evening, even if Darrel didn't want to spend the time with them. The crucial point was for Tim and Kim to give Darrel a clear message that they valued him and wouldn't let other commitments crowd him out of their lives.

If you can, try to find regular times when your teen gets your un-divided attention. Don't be put off if he seems indifferent or reluctant to join you when you first start offering your time. He may be suspicious, or trying to protect himself from possible disappointment or rejection. Don't take this personally: just continue to make yourself available.

1   Develop values

Many young people stumble during the teenage years because they are swayed by outside influences before their mature identity has emerged. You can help your teen to anchor himself by establishing strong values and generating a sense of direction for the future. These will help keep him on course as he navigates the teenage years, and encourage a positive self-image.

Teenagers are constantly evaluating their world, testing everything around them, as they try to figure out what they can rely on and the values they should invest in. That's why the clear boundaries you set around your teen's behaviour are a vital reflection of your commitment to your own value system. Teenagers will start to take their moral bearings from your reaction to their choices and attitudes, so it is important to be clear about the issues you choose to take a stand on, and why.

Whatever your teen sees and experiences will become benchmarks for her. Even if she seems oblivious to you, be aware that your behaviour is under scrutiny, and don't underestimate the influence of your example. If you and your partner argue in front of your children, they will accept this as normal. If you roll up late for appointments, don't expect your children to value punctuality. If you want your teen to take on board your values, try to live up to them yourself.

You can also help your teen to establish firmer values by talking through situations he has found challenging, or by discussing important or topical events. A family meal can be a good setting for these kinds of conversation. Help your teen to think through the issues and reach his own conclusions rather than forcing your opinions on him.

2 Inspire dreams

Teenagers often appear cynical and disillusioned. For many this is a reaction to feeling daunted by an uncertain future. If they convince themselves that everything is rubbish, they don't have to try to make anything of themselves or their lives. They can bury their heads in the moment and try not to look too far ahead.

This attitude can be stressful for parents, who are well aware that choices made in adolescence can affect the future, especially if your teenager is missing school. So it's important to support your teen by helping him create a positive vision of his future and plan a way of achieving it.

The first step is to encourage your teenager to dream. Then help her begin to map out how she can turn dreams into reality. But before you begin, remember that your teen is pursuing her dreams, not yours. Some parents get angry or disappointed because their child wants something different from what they would choose for her. Remember whose life it is.

The key is not to push, but to watch out for signs of natural interest in something, and then to nurture that enthusiasm. Even if it seems unrealistic to you, don't put your teen off. What she needs to hear from you is that life is rich in possibilities. If your daughter announces she wants to be a TV presenter or pop star, avoid saying that it will never happen, and instead do something practical to support her ambitions. If you buy your son an electric guitar, he may not end up on stage at Wembley, but he may develop a skill that he continues to enjoy into his adult years. Experience will ultimately teach him where his limits lie and let him know if he needs to adjust his dreams.

Sometimes an idea needs to be made more concrete before it can become a real dream. Look out for opportunities that allow your teen to explore her ambitions, or try out related skills. Fourteen-year-old Gemma Taylor had always been fascinated by forensic science, but it was not until a trip to a local forensic unit gave her the chance to analyse a blood splatter and lift a real footprint that she thought seriously about her dreams. She realized there were practical steps she would have to take to make her dream happen, and that the first of these was to get herself back into mainstream school.

Don't be afraid to draw upon your own experience as a way of showing your teen what is possible. When Julie Hunt opened up to her son Robert and talked about her own teenage years, she gave him a new perspective on how she had turned her life around, and he was surprised to hear that she had fulfilled one of her youthful dreams of joining a circus. Julie revealed how hard she had had to work to achieve her true ambitions. 'I've got more respect for her now,' said Robert later. 'She went back to college; there is a lot more to her.' Just remember that sharing your experience is not the same as lecturing about it.

3 Map the future

Fifteen-year-old Robert needed to build a stronger sense of his own identity to help him stand up to peer pressure and avoid trouble when out with his gang. To help him work out more clearly who he was and what he wanted from life he was encouraged to complete a 'treasure map'. He stuck a photo of himself in the middle of a sheet of paper, then collected words and images from magazines and the internet that represented all the things he valued or felt drawn to: these included the words 'family' and 'sport', as well as pictures of musicians he admired and beautiful women. He then made them into a collage, placing the images he felt most strongly attracted to nearest his own portrait. After this exercise he said, 'My ambition is to become a lawyer or take my drama further.'

Although this exercise is essentially a light-hearted one, it can be a helpful way of working out what really matters to your teen. Some teenagers are surprised when their map ends up looking quite different from what they expected. A personal treasure map can also be a 'work in progress': new items can be added and existing ones moved or exchanged as values and tastes change over time. It can serve as a helpful reminder of positive goals for the future.

If you feel bold, you and your teen can work alongside each other while you each create your individual maps. However, make sure you don't judge your teen's efforts: if it's all flash cars and supermodels, let him dream. The map is ultimately a personal creation and you should feel flattered if he is prepared to share his private hopes and dreams with you.

4 Get assertive

Teens with a poor self-image may be shy or self-conscious and find it hard to stand up for themselves; assertiveness and positive self-esteem go hand in hand. Teaching your teen how to be assertive can be a useful way of helping her to resist negative influences, as well as showing her how to get what she needs without resorting to aggression or manipulation.

It's important not to confuse assertiveness with aggression. Some teens who feel inadequate may act in a domineering way to cover up how they really feel. Being assertive means being able stand up for your own needs and rights, while also respecting the feelings of others.

Thirteen-year-old James Ellis wasn't shy, but he had difficulty expressing what it was he wanted from his family, and lacked the skills to get his wishes taken seriously. He was very frustrated, but his grumpy manner and tone of voice often worked against him. 'Nobody ever makes anything fun,' he said about family life. 'If everyone's talking, if I say one thing wrong, everyone attacks me!' James needed to learn how to make his voice heard and ask for what he wanted without being seen as a temperamental teen.

James wanted to spend more time with his father, Chris, but felt he was always fobbed off with a string of excuses. 'Sometimes he's sitting there doing nothing and I ask him if we can go golfing, and he says, "Maybe later". Maybe later always turns out to be no. Nobody really listens,' James said. Chris later admitted that he often felt too tired to give James the attention he wanted, and that his son's constant grouching made him even more reluctant to do so. As this pattern continued, James was starting to believe that his father didn't care and was getting even grumpier.

Rather than go on playing the victim, James had to learn that he could turn the situation round. He was challenged to get his father to agree to go golfing with him by being assertive, while remaining calm as the same time. This is how he went about it:

○ First he had to consider whether his request was reasonable so that he felt on firm ground when he approached his father.

○ He had to be very specific about what he wanted – in this case, getting his father to agree to go golfing.

○ He had to concentrate on expressing his own needs clearly by asking 'When can I go golfing with you?', rather than complaining that Chris always said no.

○ He had to acknowledge his father's position of being busy and tired, while still not giving up on his aim. James suggested they went golfing at the weekend.

○ Finally, he had to be persistent. When Chris tried to laugh off James's request, James had to restate his position as many times as necessary: 'I really want to go golfing with you, Dad,' until Chris agreed and a date was written on the calendar.

Chris was initially taken aback by James's new, assertive approach, but agreed that it had made his chances of success far more likely. 'Normally, if he didn't get what he wanted, regardless of the circumstances, he would immediately go into a stress,' Chris reflected.

Sisters Lucie and Elane Parkinson also used a more assertive approach to deal with their unspoken resentment towards their father, Tom, whom they felt had blown hot and cold towards them since his split from their mother when they were toddlers. They felt he never put them first, and took no interest in their lives, but their sense of hurt about this had prevented the girls from ever being able to tackle the issue directly. Instead they made demands on him for clothes and money, and continued to feel unhappy.

The girls were helped to tell Tom what they really felt, which meant taking the risk of showing him both their positive and negative feelings. Their message was simple: although they loved their father, they felt abandoned by him. 'We feel like we come third place in your life,' they told him. 'We don't know how you feel about us.' When they managed to express their feelings directly without an argument Tom was stunned, and was able to tell them how much he loved them. 'This is the best conversation we've had in years without anyone having a go at each other,' he said afterwards.

As he didn't feel attacked, Tom was able to meet the girls halfway. Plans were made for increased phone contact and regular trips out. Rather than raking over the past, the three of them were able to negotiate a blueprint for the future. The air had been cleared and the girls both felt stronger for being able to speak their minds.

Beat anger

Everyone gets angry at times, but typical teenage moodiness can easily spiral out of control. Your teen's rage may be hard for you to deal with, but it will also be affecting him: it is difficult to feel good about yourself if you are constantly losing it. That's why it's important to find ways of preventing your teen from erupting, as well as constructive ways of dealing with it if he does.

For 16-year-old Suraj De the simplest conversation with his mother could provoke him into a rage. 'When I'm that angry I just don't care and I can't help it,' he said. But Suraj had to learn that the only power his mother had to affect his level of stress was the power he gave her. His reactions were under his own control.

The first step is to help your teenager to recognize that feeling angry is not the problem. Anger is a natural emotion that can protect us and motivate us to confront injustice. But what is frequently unacceptable is the intensity of a teenager's rage and the way she expresses it. While you shouldn't tell your teen what to feel, you can encourage her to handle her feelings better. Below are some ways of tackling this.

1 Don't bottle it up

Teens who are not good at expressing their emotions tend to let anger build and then finally explode when something relatively minor proves to be the final straw. This can be mystifying to the parent, who is left thinking, 'But I only asked him to walk the dog...', unaware that they have just been served with a week's worth of pent-up fury. Encourage your teen to express feelings directly when he gets frustrated or cross rather than sitting on them and letting the pressure build.

2 Spot the warning signs

The key to managing anger effectively is to deal with it quickly *before* it gets out of hand. Teach your teen to recognize the situations likely to provoke his anger, and to spot his personal warning signs that an emotional storm is brewing. These can include particular thoughts and feelings, or physical sensations, such as butterflies in the stomach, bands of tension across the forehead, a faster heart rate or changes in breathing.

3 Take five

Just as Anni and Marie Ellis had to learn that it was vital to walk away from each other when one of their rows was brewing, you can teach your teen to call a halt to a conversation as soon as he spots the warning signs and, if necessary, take himself out of the situation for a few minutes.

If your teenager often loses his temper with you, agree a sign between you at which you will immediately take a break. When he does ask for time to cool down, it is really important that you respond supportively to his request and leave him on his own. If your teen is asking for breathing space, this is usually an encouraging sign that he is trying to regain composure. Unless you genuinely believe he is out of control and about to do something crazy, you should respect his wishes.

When Jennie Manson rushed in from the garden after a violent argument with her friends she was so worked up that her parents Ian and Tina were concerned about what she might do. Although Jennie was shouting 'Leave me alone!', their efforts to calm her down merely provoked her further and ended up with her hurling abuse at the whole family. Jennie's temper was holding everyone to ransom, so at that point the best thing her parents could have done was withdraw and let her calm down.

4 Use distraction

If your teen's anger is building, she can try to distract herself by counting down slowly from ten to one or using a relaxation technique (see opposite). If you find a way of introducing a delay before she reaches boiling point, the intensity of the anger is more likely to subside.

When your teenager becomes really stressed it can be hard for him to think of constructive ways to handle his feelings on the spot. It may help to create a personalized 'coping bank'. Gemma Taylor decorated a shoebox and put into it 20 suggestions for things she might do when she felt destructive or aggressive. The suggestions ranged from 'Making something' to 'Phoning a friend' and 'Listening to music'. When she felt stressed Gemma simply had to reach into her box and do what it said on the slip of paper she pulled out. This gave her practical ways to occupy herself when her feelings threatened to spin out of control.

Another useful trick if your teen finds herself in a situation of conflict is to suggest she imagine herself looking down on the scene from above. This simple shift in perspective can help her feel more detached and rational.

5 Keep breathing

Suraj De learnt that using breathing techniques could be a useful way of retaining control when his temper started to rise. When we are agitated our breathing rate increases to take oxygen to our muscles in preparation for either a fight or a speedy escape. By deliberately breathing slowly and calmly from the diaphragm (so he could feel his stomach expanding rather than his chest), Suraj was encouraging his body to stand down from red alert.

6 Help your teen to relax

Relaxation is a skill that needs to be learnt. If your relationship with your teenager is strong enough, encourage him to try out the following simple techniques so he can put himself into a relaxed state when he needs to. You might also like to try them for yourself.

RELAXATION TECHNIQUES

○ Sit or lie comfortably. Concentrate on your feet. Tense them as tightly as you can for a few seconds, then release them. As you do so, tell yourself: 'My feet are becoming warm and heavy'. Work your way through your body, tensing and releasing the different muscle groups until your body feels completely relaxed.

○ Picture an hourglass with red sand running from the top globe into the bottom one. Imagine that the sand represents your anger and stress draining away, and keep visualizing the hourglass until all the sand has run through. If need be, repeat the exercise until you feel at ease.

○ In your mind's eye picture a location in which you feel completely relaxed, happy and secure. This can be a real place, or one you create using your imagination. Work up the image using your five senses. What can you see around you? Can you smell the sea air? Can you feel the warmth of the sun on your back? Once you feel relaxed, think of one word that sums up the whole scene. As you repeat the word to yourself, bring your thumb and first finger together. Do this five minutes a night just before sleep on a regular basis. Eventually, simply by bringing your thumb and index finger together and repeating the word silently in your head you will be able conjure up a calmer state of mind when you feel under pressure. It really does work, but practice is the key.

7 Get physical

Physical exercise is a great way to relieve stress and burn off tension. For some teenagers having a specific physical outlet for their aggression can diffuse anger. Some parents find that a punch-bag helps teenagers to vent their stress; for others this simply winds them up further. Sports such as boxing or martial arts, which teach self-discipline and the controlled release of aggression, can also be effective. Sixteen-year-old Roy Taylor was encouraged to try out the martial art aikido, which taught him a whole new approach to situations where he felt attacked. He was fascinated to learn that the body is actually much stronger when relaxed than when it is in a state of tension.

POINTS TO REMEMBER

○ Working on your teen's self-esteem will help protect her from the troubled behaviour that often characterizes people who don't value themselves.

○ The teenage years are a time of many doubts; help prevent your teen from developing a self-critical inner voice.

○ Develop your relationship with your teenager by giving plenty of time, encouragement and support, which will make her feel good about herself.

○ Show where your boundaries are to help your teenager develop values. Lead by example.

○ Inspire your teen both to have dreams and to follow them. Help him to create a positive vision of his future and find ways of achieving it.

○ Help your teen learn to stand up for her rights and ask for what she needs by being calmly assertive.

○ Anger might make your teenager feel negative about herself. Teach her that there are ways of controlling and managing anger that may help her avoid conflict.

○ Teach your teen positive relaxation techniques as a way of keeping stress and anger at bay.

chapter eight

Family matters

EVERY FAMILY HAS ITS OWN UNIQUE SET OF EXPERIENCES. FAMILY LIFE CAN BE exhilarating, but it is also often highly demanding, and each family needs to face the constant challenge of adapting to change. One reason why the teenage years can be so turbulent is that the pressures of adolescence often coincide with major changes taking place in the lives of other family members.

By the time your child hits his teens, you may be facing mid-life issues of your own – from career or relationship changes to looking after increasingly elderly parents. You may have other older or younger children going through a variety of their own life stages – from getting married to starting school. With so much going on, it can be hard to keep your eye on the ball and prevent even normal levels of teen behaviour from putting a strain on the family.

All your family relationships and the ways in which they interact can have an impact on your teen's behaviour, so it is important to be aware of how your family is working, and to find ways of resolving any conflict between you. This could mean revisiting conflict that has taken place in the past and finding new ways of resolving it before you and your teenager can move on.

United we stand

While making *Teen Angels*, we met many parents who were as frustrated with each other as they were with their teens. It is not always easy to work together as parents, but since teenagers are so good at exploiting the differences between their parents, it is important to find ways of supporting each other as much as possible. Different approaches to parenting, contrasting teenage experiences of your own and stressful work patterns can all contribute to bad feeling between you, and leave partners feeling unsupported or criticized.

1 Be supportive

When Luke Gibson described his mother as 'f***ed in the head' his father Rob didn't express any surprise – he just agreed with his son that Glynis needed to 'chill out more'. With both parents struggling to contain their sons' loutish behaviour, this was not the message that Luke needed to hear from his father. Don't undermine the other parent by allowing your teen to treat them disrespectfully, and don't let your teen see you being disrespectful either.

If you do feel your partner is being unsupportive, the first step is to talk about it. When Dawn Taylor revealed that she often felt unsupported by her husband 'Big' Roy in dealing with their two teenagers, Roy and Gemma, he admitted that he often left discipline to his wife because he was frightened that his explosive temper might make the situation worse. This, however, left Dawn fighting many battles on her own, and it was wearing her down.

The Taylors found a way forward by using the 'Big Roy' technique. When 14-year-old Gemma started behaving badly or trying to play one parent off against the other, Big Roy and Dawn would simply ignore her while they talked directly and calmly to each other about how they intended to deal with the situation. They could then clearly and calmly tell her what they wanted her to do. It was a turning point for both parents: Roy discovered that he could get involved without losing his temper, and Dawn no longer felt left without back-up. As an added bonus, Gemma realized that she would not get attention from her parents while she was being disruptive.

2 Check in with each other

When John Pauley came in from work and awarded 15-year-old Dominic extra time on the computer after his mother Nia had already asked him to stop, Nia decided that she would pull the plug anyway. Naturally this caused friction between Dominic and his mother, as well as between Nia and John. If John had taken a few moments to check in with his wife, he might have prevented a situation that made them appear divided, and cast Nia in the role of 'bad cop'.

Openly disagreeing with your partner about discipline in front of your teenager can be a recipe for disaster. While working as a team does not mean that you have to agree on everything, if you find yourself at odds with your partner, it's best to signal that you need to discuss it in private, where you can reach a quiet compromise. Otherwise your teen will quickly learn which of you is most likely to take her side, and exploit the situation to her advantage.

If you are facing a tricky discipline issue with your teen, don't feel pressurized to react straight away. While younger children won't get the message unless they are able to connect your response with their actions, this is not true of teenagers. If anything, keeping your teen in a state of suspense while he awaits your joint verdict will underline that you are taking the issue seriously. It is far better to wait and come up with the right sanction that you have discussed with your partner than to charge in and later be left feeling that you could have handled the situation better another way.

3 Put your heads together

'I can't ever once remember one single time of my mum and dad being together, not even in the same room,' sobbed 17-year-old Lucie Parkinson. 'It makes me feel like I'm missing out because all of my mates have had that.' Lucie's parents had been divorced since she and her sister Elane were very small; since then the parents had had nothing to do with each other. But the lack of communication between them was still having an effect on their daughters many years later.

Lucie and Elane would exploit their parents' lack of unity by fleeing to their dad Tom's house whenever they fell out with their mother

Helen. Tom would welcome them unquestioningly, leaving Helen feeling frustrated and disempowered. But when Tom and Helen were persuaded to meet face to face for the first time in 14 years, Tom was surprised to discover how much this situation was affecting his ex-wife. Tom and Helen agreed some rules about how he would deal with the girls turning up at his house, and, more importantly, they decided to meet regularly to discuss the girls' progress. 'I'd like to get to know a bit more about the girls, about their school,' Tom realized. By forming a better alliance, both parents felt more confident in their relationship with their daughters.

Even if you are not living with your teen's mother or father, it's important to take time out together to discuss your child. This gives you a chance to review how you have handled situations that have already happened, and to plan ahead and anticipate any potential problems. If you are able to spot likely problems up front and work out your strategies for dealing with them, your teenager will be less able to play you off against each other.

For many couples a regular outing on their own is the best way of thinking things through. Nia and John Pauley agreed to have a weekly session at their local pub, where they could spend some time together away from their teenage sons and identify any problems that they needed to address.

4 Be a parent, not a best mate

John Pauley and his son Dominic got on like a house on fire; so well, in fact, that mother Nia often found herself left out in the cold. When Dominic casually announced to his dad that his mother had asked him to tidy his room but he 'couldn't be bothered' to do it, John's failure to pick him up on this remark spoke volumes. The alliance between father and son may have been strengthened, but at the cost of Nia's authority as a parent. However proud you may be of your relationship with your teen, you must always make sure that your bond doesn't compromise his relationship with your fellow parent. As a parent, you may sometimes have to make yourself unpopular to get the job done.

Try to ensure that your teenagers recognize you as a parental unit, as well as separate individuals. If you are living together, make time to do things together to strengthen your own relationship, and present yourselves as a couple in your teens' eyes. Talk through issues so that you can present a united front with confidence when you need to.

If you have a close relationship with your teen, it can be tempting to confide in her too much, or use her as a sounding-board for problems in your relationship with her other parent. This is best avoided, as it is unfair on both your teen and your partner, and can cause friction.

If you are separated, avoid criticizing the absent parent, however aggrieved you may feel. Your teen will draw his own conclusions in time, but will struggle if he finds himself caught in a conflict of loyalty and feels under pressure to agree with your point of view.

You're not my real dad

'She doesn't realize how much it hurts to be told "You're not my dad",' confided Ian Manson about his stepdaughter Jennie. 'I've been her dad for 14 years. I've never hidden the fact that I'm not her biological father, but in every other way I've treated her as my daughter.' As the only father Jennie had ever known, Ian was devastated when she turned biology against him in the heat of the moment when they had a physical fight. He didn't appreciate that Jennie was simply trying to hurt him with the best weapon she could find.

In Europe 25 per cent of children will have experienced the divorce of their parents by the time they are 16. With the divorce rate steadily climbing, many children, by the time they reach their teenage years, will find themselves living in families in which one or both parents may have remarried or moved in with a new partner.

Finding yourself in the position of step-parent can be daunting, particularly if the children you take on have a strong attachment to the absent biological parent. Working out how to earn the children's respect and how far your authority extends can be a challenge.

But just because you have no genetic connection to the children doesn't mean that your partner's offspring can ignore you or treat you badly. At the very least you are an adult who deserves to be treated respectfully as the partner of their biological parent. You are also a member of the household who will probably still be there once the children have left. You may even own part or all of the property in which your partner's children are living. All these factors give you certain rights, and you should protect them.

There are no hard and fast rules. Your role in the life of any teens you have taken on will depend on a number of factors: the length of time you have been with their mother or father, the role of the absent biological parent, and the willingness of the natural parent you live with to involve you in parenting issues. It is usually best to take the lead from the biological parent, but the more you can play an active supporting role and work at developing your own relationship with your partner's children, the better.

'I wouldn't allow my own child to behave like that,' David Hunt said of his 15-year-old stepson Robert. But he felt his hands were tied because Robert wasn't his own son, and his view of him was frequently negative. Robert's mother Julie learnt that she needed to give David permission to parent Robert; in return, David realized that to support Julie he needed to adopt a more positive attitude and stop feeding into her worst fears about her son. David's efforts didn't go unnoticed. 'He is a lot more supportive, instead of putting me down,' revealed Robert.

Sibling strife

Half-child, half-adult, teenagers are quite capable of behaving like both at times. Sometimes your teen will retreat from the pressures of adolescence into childlike behaviour, and nowhere is this more obvious than in his relationship with his siblings.

Sisters Lucie and Elane Parkinson were constantly fighting. Their screeching battles were mostly over clothes and make-up, but in reality their perpetual state of warfare reflected the insecurity and rivalries of much younger children. The sisters were really vying for their mum Helen's time and attention, and they were prepared to do whatever was necessary to see off their rival.

Since teenagers can seem so grown up and fiercely independent, it is easy to forget that they do still need your attention, however dismissive they may appear to be. It is especially easy to neglect them when you have younger siblings who have much more immediate needs.

It was apparent that 13-year-old Darrel Patterson felt he was being squeezed out by his two-year-old half-brother Rowen. As his mother and stepdad sat around the table delighting in 'what a good boy' Rowen was, Darrel's face was like thunder. The situation could have been helped by developing Darrel's role as elder brother and giving him more responsibility for Rowen's care. But because Darrel's behaviour had become unpredictable, his parents Kim and Tim felt uneasy about leaving Darrel in charge.

Some teens are better at getting their parents' attention than others. Thirteen-year-old James Pauley used to strengthen his position as his mother Nia's favourite by taking on the role of the 'third parent' in the family, and letting her know when 15-year-old Dominic was up to no good. This might have made James and Nia closer, but it was having a negative effect on his relationship with his older brother. It's important to discourage this kind of rivalry, as it could be storing up trouble for the future.

Dominic also felt aggrieved that James was getting away with things because he had some special needs. James actually admitted that he sometimes used his apparent vulnerability to manipulate his parents. But by giving in to James and not making him face up to the consequences of his actions, parents Nia and John were unwittingly making it harder for the boys to get along, as well as possibly affecting James's ability to act more maturely.

Teenage siblings will often use each other as convenient 'whipping boys' to work out frustrations and resentments from other areas of their life. Fourteen-year-old Gemma Taylor and her 16-year-old brother Roy were close in many ways, but this didn't stop them from getting into terrible fights. Roy's philosophy was that any opponent of his needed to be pummelled until they were well and truly crushed. As he used to practise on his sister, Gemma learnt to see herself as tough too, and started initiating fights outside the home. Gemma and Roy were encouraged to give up play-fighting because they were unable to control how far it went, and it was affecting the atmosphere at home. Make sure you don't tolerate any behaviour under your own roof that you would label as 'bullying' or unacceptably violent outside the home.

Trying to make sure that you treat siblings fairly does not mean that they have to be treated identically. The goal is to ensure that the needs of all your children are being met, bearing in mind that these may be different for each individual. However, it is important that your teens feel they are being treated equally, particularly when it comes to discipline. Try to create family rules that have equivalent consequences for your different children. The Pauley family agreed that 13-year-old James would lose his extra staying-up time at weekends if he failed to complete his chores, while 15-year-old Dominic would forgo his extra computer time.

Moving on

All families go through difficult times, and some level of conflict is both inevitable and normal. But sometimes things happen that are never properly resolved, and when the immediate drama fades, issues get swept under the carpet. The problem with this is that buried resentments tend to resurface, sometimes taking new and unpredictable turns.

Whether you are facing a conflict based on a current situation, or recognize that a past situation is continuing to have an effect on your relationship with your teen, it is worth taking steps to resolve the issue properly. These steps are outlined below.

1 Make it safe to talk

If you are going to discuss a difficult issue with your teen, try to establish some ground rules for the conversation so that everyone can feel secure. When 16-year-old Anni Ellis faced the difficult prospect of confessing to her parents Marie and Chris that she had been skipping school, it was crucial that they remained calm and gave Anni space to speak without interrupting. Similarly, Lesley and Peter Maddison Stokes had to keep a lid on their own anxiety and disappointment when 16-year-old Tom chose to be honest with them about his problems with dope smoking.

If your teen is brave enough to open up to you, remember that the stakes are high. If you react badly at these times, she may never take the risk again. If you feel you are about to lose control for any reason, it is better that you simply thank your teen for sharing with you and say that you need some time to digest what has been said. This way you will be able to pick up the conversation when you feel ready.

2 Don't be fobbed off

Teenagers tend to feel things deeply and will sometimes become defensive when you try to raise issues that have really wounded them. It can be tempting to let things lie, but it's better if you persist by continuing to raise the topic gently. You can allow your teen to close down the conversation if it all becomes too much, but you will usually find that in time she will respond.

Fifteen-year-olds Luke and Jonny Gibson had been partially raised by their grandparents, before both died within a short space of time. The boys were resistant to talking about how their grandparents' deaths had affected them, so it was not discussed within the family. But everyone was affected. 'I'm a lost soul without Mum and Dad, without having them in the background,' said the twins' mother, Glynis.

When Jonny was eventually persuaded to open up he agreed that his grandparents' deaths had had 'a big effect on everyone'. If they were still alive, he observed, 'me and Luke would be up at Nanna and Grandad's all the time – and they'd be very disappointed in the stuff that we've done'. Instead he felt that he and Luke had no one to support them, as Glynis was often at work and did a lot of night shifts. 'If her job wasn't a problem, there'd be no problem in the house,' he claimed.

Glynis finally had to acknowledge that her way of coping with her own sense of loss and helplessness had been to bury herself in work. 'I just wish my mum was here for me now because if the boys feel I'm not there for them, then I know how they feel. And I feel a bit of a failure,' she admitted. Glynis changed her working hours so that she could be around at home more, and the twins' behaviour began to improve. By facing the issue rather than avoiding it, the family was able to reunite and come to terms with the buried grief that had driven them apart.

3 Be honest and admit your mistakes

After weeks of cold-shouldering each other in the aftermath of their physical fight, Jennie and Ian Manson were finally ready to make up. Rather than blaming each other, they followed an important principle for resolving deep-seated conflicts by writing each other a letter giving an honest account of their feelings. In his letter Ian apologized, admitting that it had been wrong of him to hit Jennie, and promising that it wouldn't happen again. He was candid enough to say, 'Even if I don't particularly like you at times, you will always be my daughter and I love you.'

'It will take time to rebuild trust and respect,' wrote Jennie. 'Now I feel more comfortable spending time with you.' But, most importantly, she admitted: 'I know I've said you aren't, but you *are* my dad, and I'm very grateful for all you've done for me, you've given me a decent life.' This approach was far more realistic than pretending that their differences had been magically swept away. Some hurts take time to heal, and successful reconciliation can only take place a step at a time.

Don't be afraid to admit when you are in the wrong. Some parents feel that they will lose their teens' respect if they acknowledge their own faults, but usually the reverse is true. Your teen will be only too well aware of them in any case, and a timely apology can work wonders

4 Address hidden issues

When Julie Hunt decided to brave a long overdue conversation with her son Robert about the effects of the past, she knew exactly what she needed to say. As a younger child, Robert had repeatedly intervened to protect her from a violent partner. Although Robert declared that he didn't want to discuss it, Julie insisted. 'I want you to listen. I want to say thank you. I know how much you protected me and looked out for me, and I want to say it's OK – you don't have to look after me any more.' By making it clear to Robert that she was no longer the vulnerable woman that she had been back then, Julie was releasing Robert from any sense of obligation that he needed to look after her now.

Placing himself as his mother's protector meant that Robert had never been able to deal with his own hurt. Instead he had run away from his confused feelings by hooking up with his teenage gang, in whose company he could act out some of his anger and frustration. Julie wanted Robert to understand that he didn't need to feel he should carry and protect his friends in the same way he had protected her. 'You shouldn't have to carry anyone,' Julie told him. 'You're only responsible for yourself.' In a sense, Julie was setting him free. Now it was time for Robert to move on.

POINTS TO REMEMBER

❍ It is important to be united with your partner in parenting your teenager. Don't let your teen play you off against each other.

❍ Check in with your partner before you discipline your teen to make sure that you share the same approach.

❍ Take the time to review how you are parenting your teenagers by spending time alone with your partner. If you are separated from your teenager's other parent, continue to look for ways of communicating about your child.

❍ If you are a step-parent, play an active supporting role and ensure that you are getting respect from your partner's teens. Take your lead from your partner when it comes to discipline issues.

❍ Try to treat all siblings fairly. Be aware that much sibling rivalry is designed to get your attention.

❍ Help your teenager move on from difficulties in your family's past by keeping communication open.

❍ If you have conflicts to resolve, do so honestly. Be prepared to admit your mistakes, and help your teenager to move on from hers.

And finally...

IF YOU ARE STRUGGLING WITH YOUR TEEN, HANG ON IN THERE. REMIND YOURSELF that the worst of the teenage years are soon over, and the majority of teenagers do eventually become responsible members of society, however challenging their behaviour may be for you now.

One thing to remember if you have a teenager is that bigger changes are just around the corner. However deeply you try to bury the knowledge, one implication of your child's first outbreak of spots is that it won't be very long before he's an adult and poised to leave home.

In the meantime, the teenage years are crucial ones for your child, as new opportunities present themselves and horizons open up before him. Whenever you feel that parenting a teenager is a thankless task, remind yourself that your commitment to doing the best for your teen represents a genuine investment in his future. If you stand by him during this sometimes tricky phase of his development, you will also be laying a solid foundation for your future relationship with him as an adult.

We hope that some of the advice in this book helps you to plot a surer course as you navigate your way through the often troubled teenage years. We wish you and your own Teen Angels the very best of luck!

Further information

Please note that some of the organizations listed below offer only online support or information; where phone numbers are not supplied, telephone contact is not available.

Support for parents

Gingerbread
Tel: 0800 018 4318
www.gingerbread.org.uk
A national charity that offers support and assistance to lone-parent families.

Parentline Plus
Tel: 0808 800 2222
www.parentlineplus.org.uk
A UK-registered charity offering information and emotional support to families.

Pink Parents
Tel: 08701 273 274
www.pinkparents.org.uk
Offers a range of support services and social activities for lesbian, gay, bisexual and transgendered parents.

Raising Kids
Tel: 020 8444 4852
www.raisingkids.co.uk
Offers support, information and friendship to everyone raising kids – from babies to teens.

Relate
Tel: 0845 456 1310
www.relate.org.uk
The UK's largest and most experienced relationship counselling organization. Relate can help families, parents and young people with relationship problems.

Further information and advice on a wide range of subjects can be found on the BBC Parenting website: www.bbc.co.uk/parenting

Support for teens
Connexions
Tel: 0808 001 3219
www.connexions.gov.uk
Information and advice for 13–19-year-olds on a range of subjects, including health, relationships, learning, careers, leaving home and money.

Helping Teens
www.helpingteens.org
A peer-to-peer support network for teens, including support group forums, email support, live chat, and articles on diverse topics, including friendship, school, sexuality, suicide, job-hunting, smoking and much more.

Need 2 Know
www.need2know.co.uk
Information portal for teenagers, with an online magazine and links to other useful websites. Sections include health, relationships, money, travel and the law.

Subject-related sites

Bullying

Bullying Online

www.bullying.co.uk

The Anti-Bullying Campaign website, giving advice to parents and children, and suggestions for schools.

Childline

Tel: 0800 1111

www.childline.org.uk

Free helpline for children and young people in the UK. Telephone counsellors can help with any problem, including bullying.

Kidscape

Tel: 020 7730 3300; Helpline: 08451 205 204

www.kidscape.org.uk

Advice on the prevention of bullying and child abuse.

Drugs and alcohol

Addaction

www.youngaddaction.org.uk

Offers advice to young people and families dealing with drug and alcohol misuse. Regional contact numbers are available on the website.

Adfam

Tel: 020 7928 8898

www.adfam.org.uk

The families' alcohol and drugs agency offers information about legal issues, as well as an online message board and database of local support groups.

D-world
Tel: 020 7928 1211
www.drugscope.org.uk
Aimed at 11–14-year-olds, this website includes information on the law and how to stay safe, as well as games and personal testimonies.

Home Office
Tel: 020 7035 4848
www.homeoffice.gov.uk
This government website has a section on drugs, with useful advice on young people's drug use, plus further links.

Talk to Frank
Tel: 0800 77 66 00
www.talktofrank.com
Good site for both teens and parents, offering free, confidential drugs information and advice, 24 hours a day.

Wrecked
www.wrecked.co.uk
Alcohol information aimed at young people. Includes quizzes, personal stories, and a check-your-units test.

Eating disorders

Eating Disorders Association
Tel: 0845 634 7650 (Youthline – up to and including 18 years of age); 0845 634 1414 (Adult Helpline for those over 18)
www.edauk.com
Offers support for sufferers and relevant links.

Something Fishy
www.something-fishy.org
A strangely named but useful site, with information and strategies for spotting and tackling eating disorders, as well as supporting sufferers.

Mental health

EQUIP (Electronic Quality Information for Patients)

Tel: 0121 414 7754

www.equip.nhs.uk/groups/teenager.html

NHS site offering links to a variety of useful websites on teenage issues, including mental health.

Young Minds

Tel: 020 7336 8445

www.youngminds.org.uk

A national charity committed to improving the mental health of all children and young people. Offers information on a range of mental health subjects affecting young people, including anxiety, depression, eating problems and attention deficit disorder.

Young People and Self-harm

www.selfharm.org.uk

A key information resource for young people who self-harm, their friends and families, and for professionals working with them.

Sex and contraception

Brook

Tel: 020 7284 6040

www.brook.org.uk

Provides free and confidential sexual health advice to all young people up to the age of 25. Includes information on sexual health issues, as well as contraception services.

R U Thinking About It?

Tel: 0800 28 29 30

www.ruthinking.co.uk

Teenager-friendly site providing young people under the age of 18 with information on sex, relationships and contraception, as well as links to helplines.

Acknowledgements

This book would not have been written without the huge contribution of the parents and teens who were brave enough to take part in *Teen Angels*. Their determination to change their relationships, and willingness to let cameras into their lives deserve our greatest thanks and admiration.

Our thanks also to Stuart Murphy and his team at BBC3, who have helped make all the *Angels* programmes so successful. Also to John Lynch and Reem Nouss, who were key in getting the first series on air; to Blue Ryan, Sue Learoyd and Rachel Baldwin for their fantastic support, and to Sarah Ross McClean for keeping us cost-efficient. Huge thanks go to the entire production team, whose tireless professionalism and unflagging dedication to producing the programmes has made the series such a rewarding experience for us both.

Thanks to on-screen experts Dr Tanya Byron and Laverne Antrobus for their wisdom, skill and support – and for being such good fun to work with. And also to Sarah Helps for her back-up behind the scenes.

We would also like to thank Emma Shackleton at BBC Active and our editor Trish Burgess for keeping us on track. Stephen would like to thank Kate Alexander and Jo Sarsby for sorting him out, and Sacha thanks Nena Matic for all her help and support.

Special love and gratitude to Mel Briers and Duncan Ackery, whose patience, encouragement and dedication to the cause of lone parenting over many long, wet weekends have made the writing of this book possible. And finally – to Joe, Will, Evie, Tom and Teddy, our teenagers in waiting. We're ready!

The *Teen Angels* team

Executive Producers: Reem Nouss, Sacha Baveystock (series producer Series 1)

Series Producer: Blue Ryan (line producer Series 1)

Line Producers: Sue Learoyd, Rachel Baldwin

Directors: Ruth Whippman, Rachel Lalljee, Helen Seaman, Stephen Maud, Nicola Matthews, Clare Lockhart, Gretchen Shoring, Libby Turner, Natalie Watts, Helen Shariatmadari, Rachel Scarrott, Fiona Inskip

Assistant Producers: Daniel Bays, Melanie Heath, Sally Rose, Claire Messenger, Nishi Bolakee, Sarah Webster, Hayley Sarian, Juliet Singer, Alex Sunderland, Olivia Abrahams, Cynthia Charles

Researchers: Francesca Palmer, Jess Gillman, Victoria Atkinson, Cat Cubie, Tom Currie, Michelle Milner

Production Manager: Sarah Ross McClean

Production Team: James Vale, Karen Bonnici, Shelley Raichura, Michelle Roberts, Nik Gawinowski, Ruth Lacey, Julie Wilkinson, Gemma Treeby, Gareth Morrow

On-screen Experts: Dr Stephen Briers, Dr Tanya Byron, Laverne Antrobus

Picture credits

Dorling Kindersley, page 16; Getty Images Inc, pages 32 (Penny Tweedie/Stone/Getty Images), 92 (Digital Vision / Getty Images) and 118 (Photodisc Green / Getty Images); Michael Newman/PHOTOEDIT page 68; Stockbyte, pages 6, 52 and 132.

Index

abuse, verbal 35, 38, 43–5 *passim*,
    73, 88
accusations 38–40
addictions 115, 116
admiration 29
adolescence 8, 10–12, 14, 27
advice, asking for 8, 61, 108, 116
    giving 49, 93
aggression 11, 34, 56, 61, 115, 124, 128
    verbal 38, 44–5, 77
aikido 130
alcohol 14, 93, 108–11
allowance 61–3 *passim*, 76, 77, 80–1,
    84, 85, 115
anger 13, 26, 27, 35, 43, 56, 73, 114,
    126–9
    controlling 126–30
    warning signs 127
anorexia 103–4
Antrobus, Laverne 9
anxiety 11, 14, 19, 20, 23, 98
apologizing 34, 42, 56, 87, 142
appearance 11, 102–3, 105
arguing 20, 25, 34–6 *passim*, 38–9, 44,
    70, 76
    avoiding 43–4
assertiveness 30, 54, 124–6, 130
attention 37, 63, 121, 125, 138–9
    need for 13, 20, 22, 23, 30, 139
attitudes 30, 46
avoidance, of problems 26–7, 30

backing down 26, 34
battles, choosing 15 *see also* conflicts
bedroom 57, 58, 95
    searching 58, 79, 112
    tidying 73–6 *passim*, 136
beliefs 28
bingeing 103, 105
Borstal 24, 97
boundaries 13, 25, 27, 69–90, 93, 96,
    112, 115, 121
boys 10–11, 106, 109
breaking away 12–14
breaking cycle 27–30, 44–5
breathing techniques 128–9
bribing 84

Briers, Stephen 9
'buffer zone' 73, 75
bulimia 103–4
bullying 99–100, 140
bunking off 100–2
Byron, Tania 9

cannabis 26, 57, 58, 61, 79, 111–12
careers 14, 101
child, treating like 20, 25, 96
chores, household 61–3 *passim*, 70, 76,
    78, 80, 83
clothes 94
college 19, 26, 37, 41, 57, 58
commitment 28, 145
communication 15, 27, 30, 33–50, 77,
    93, 107, 114, 125–6
    failure 33–42
    improving 44–50
    starting 46, 50
comparisons, negative 43
compliments 46–7, 63, 120
    book 29
compromise 75, 135
condoms, use of 107
confidence 28, 64, 100, 121
conflicts 8–10 *passim*, 13, 19, 20, 34,
    44, 133 *see also* fighting; rows
    family 140–3
    resolving 35
    sibling 138–40, 143
consequences 18, 41, 45, 54, 62, 64, 71,
    74, 77–81, 83, 85–9 *passim*, 116
consistency 13, 81–3 *passim*, 86–7
contract, family 70–7
    breaking 77
    involving teens 73–5
    loopholes 75–6
contributing to family life 71, 76
control 22, 30, 54, 126–9 *passim*
    loss of 17–18, 28, 35
cool, keeping your 26, 35
coping bank 128
criminal behaviour 14, 61, 84
criticism 37, 76, 120
curfew 73, 79

damage 56, 73, 88, 114
    paying for 84
De, Suraj 12, 14, 19, 25, 28, 37, 41, 42,
    48, 55, 57–9 passim, 65, 77–9 passim,
    95, 96, 110, 112–13, 115, 126, 128–9
diary, keeping 9–10, 18–22 passim, 30,
    120
diets 104, 105
disagreement between partners 135
discipline 28, 70, 87–8, 134, 135, 140, 143
distraction 128
divorce 24, 106, 135, 137
dreams 122–3, 130
drinking 9, 19, 24, 93, 109–11
    binge 26, 110
    pre- tips 111
drugs 14, 26, 53, 61, 64, 77, 79, 87, 93,
    108–9, 111–16
    alternatives to 115
    counsellor 61, 114–15
    signs of use 113
drunkenness 110, 111

eating disorders 61, 102–5
    binge 103, 105
education 12, 14 see also school
    sex 106–8
Ellis, Anni 11, 25–6, 33, 36, 98, 100–1,
    127, 140
    Chris 25, 60, 98, 125, 140
    James 9, 13, 59–60, 98, 124–5
    Marie 25, 26, 33, 36, 59–60, 98,
        100, 127, 140
emotions 26, 27, 30, 34, 39–40, 42–3,
    47, 55, 56, 63, 66, 102, 126–9
encouragement 47, 99, 121
engaging 37, 47–8, 50, 97, 121
escaping problems 26–7, 108–13
exam results 98
example, setting 56, 64, 110, 122, 130
exclusion, from school 17, 80, 88, 94,
    98, 99
exercise 130
expectations, negative 28–30 passim
    positive 29–30
experimentation 12, 14, 112
eye contact 37

failure 33–42, 64, 81
faith, keeping 28, 47, 50
family 7–9, 12, 133–43
    contract 70–7

meal 76, 122
    meetings 76–7
fashion 14
favouritism 20
fears 13–14, 25
feedback, positive 46–7, 50, 63, 76, 120
fighting 24, 34, 53, 56, 94, 96, 99,
    139–40
fines 72, 79, 85–6
freedom 13, 54, 79
friends 12, 19, 68, 94–7
    parents' view of 94–7 passim
frustration 17, 24, 26, 33, 36, 41, 99
funding 18, 80–1 see also allowance
future, mapping 123–4

gang activities 12, 24, 26, 64, 94, 95
getting up 17, 18, 40, 62, 73, 102
Gibson, Glynis 17–18, 28, 40, 45, 62,
    69–70, 72–3, 80–1, 85–6, 134, 141–2
    Jonny 17–18, 28, 40, 45, 69–70,
        72–3, 80–1, 85–6, 98, 141–2
    Luke 17–18, 28, 37–8, 45, 47–8,
        62, 69–70, 72–3, 80–1, 85–6,
        98, 134, 141–2
    Rob 17–18, 28, 37–8, 47–8, 64, 70,
        72–3, 81, 85–6, 134
girls 10–11, 106, 109
giving in 20, 45, 81, 82, 87, 139
GP 61, 108, 115
grandparents 141
grounding 37, 47, 79, 81–2, 86–7
    breaking 82, 83
    enforcing 81–2
growth, physical 10–11
guilt-tripping 42–4 passim

harming self/others 60
health problems 110, 112
help, professional 61, 114–16 passim
home 65, 66, 95–7 passim
homework 59–60, 71, 98–9
hope 29
hormones 10–11
Hull, Kim 121, 139
    Rowen 139
    Tim 98–9, 121, 139
Hunt, David 12, 24, 37, 53–4, 71–2, 94,
    138
    Julie 9, 12, 24, 47, 53–4, 64, 71,
        81, 86–7, 95, 97, 109, 123, 138,
        142–3

identity, establishing 12, 24, 30, 39, 63–4, 94, 119
inadequacy 13, 25, 43, 104, 119, 120, 124
incentive scheme 101
independence 13, 14, 94
insecurity 20, 28, 38, 43, 94, 138
insults 38, 103
internet, access 74, 79
intervening, parents 54, 60–2, 96
involving teens 71, 73–5, 89
irritability 113

Kingdon, Robert 9, 12, 24, 26, 37, 47, 53–4, 64–5, 71, 81, 86–7, 94, 95, 97, 109, 123, 138, 142–3

language 37–8, 43 see also swearing
laundry, dirty 58, 59, 62, 73, 74, 78
law, relations with 12, 84, 94, 108
learning problems 99, 101
leaving home 12–13, 61–2, 65, 88–9
letter-writing 142
letting go 64–5, 116
listening 36–7, 43, 48, 97
love 120

Maddison, Nick 62–3, 76, 81
    Tom 26, 27, 56, 61–2, 64, 71, 76, 77, 88, 111–15 passim, 141
Maddison Stokes, Lesley 56, 61–2, 71, 76, 77, 81, 88, 111, 113, 140–1
    Peter 71, 88, 140–1
Manson, Ian 23–4, 27, 34, 46–7, 70, 73, 95–6, 98, 121, 128, 137, 142
    Jennie 13, 23–4, 26, 27, 34, 36, 46–7, 56, 63, 70, 73, 75–6, 95–6, 98, 121, 128, 137, 142
    Tina 46–7, 56, 73, 126
maturity, sexual 11
meal, family 76, 122
meetings, family 76–7
mental illness 61
mind games 42
mistakes, admitting 142, 143
    learning from 55
money 61, 64, 69, 72, 80–1
    management 64
monitoring 82–3, 85
moods 11, 104, 109, 113
morality 14
motivation 22–7, 30, 75, 84, 116

lack of 112, 113
music, playing 17, 72

nagging 19, 28, 40–1, 44, 45
name-calling 38, 82, 103
needs 13–15 passim, 23, 54, 66, 139–40
    parents' 54–6, 66
negotiating 69–75

oestrogen 10
over-compensating 28

parents 14–15, 18–21, 27–30
    absent 125–6, 135–7 passim
    discussing together 83, 135–6
    and drugs 114–16
    effects of problems on 57–9, 66
    and friends of teens 94–7 passim
    needs 54–6, 66
    protection of 24, 54, 78, 88, 142–3
    reactions 10, 18, 24, 28, 30, 44, 94, 141
    relations between 134–7, 143
    relations with teens 7, 15, 64–6 passim, 88, 120–6, 130, 136–7
    rights 54–6, 58, 65, 66, 69, 78, 88
    and school 101–2
    and sex education 106–8
    unity 134–7, 143
Parkinson, Elane 11, 20, 28, 35, 36, 46, 48, 63, 102–3, 105, 120, 125–6, 135–6, 138
    Lucie 11, 13, 20, 28, 35, 36, 38–40, 46, 63, 102–3, 105, 120, 125–6, 135–6, 138
    Tom 125–6, 135–6
partying 12, 41
past, raking up 42, 44
patience 14
Patterson, Darrel 83–4, 95, 98–9, 102, 121, 139
Pauley, Dominic 25, 73–4, 110, 135, 136, 140
    James 25, 73–4, 99, 139, 140
    John 25, 73–4, 135, 136, 139
    Nia 73–4, 135, 136, 139
peer groups 11, 14, 24, 94–7, 103
    pressure 14, 24, 87, 94–5, 99, 106–9 passim, 123
periods 10, 11
persistence 30, 48, 86, 125
perspective, shift in 128

piercing body 94, 95
pleading 18, 41
points to remember 15, 30, 49–50, 66,
    89–90, 130, 143
police 34, 53, 79, 84, 86, 113
positive, getting 29–30
power 25–6
powerlessness 13, 56, 93
praise 24, 47, 87, 120
    lack of 23, 46, 48
pregnancy 107, 108
pressure 10, 11, 26, 93–116, 133
    peer 14, 24, 87, 94–5, 99, 106–9
    passim, 123
principles 33–42, 71, 72, 75, 78
privileges 79–80
problems, effects of 57–9
protection, of parent 24, 54, 78, 88,
    142–3
puberty 10–11
punchbag 130
punishment 42, 47, 80, 83–4, 86, 87

questions 42, 44, 48–50 passim

reactions, of parents 10, 18, 24, 28, 30,
    44, 94, 141
reasoning 35, 78
reassurance, need for 13, 24, 30
recklessness 12
reconciliation 142
rejection 13, 121
relationships, family 133–43
    with parents 7, 15, 64–6 passim,
        88, 120–6, 130, 136–7
    between parents 134–7, 143
    between siblings 138–40
relaxing 48, 128–30
    techniques 129
resentment 25, 125–6, 140
respect 18, 27, 34–5, 65, 71, 75, 78,
    123, 142
    lack of 34–5
response 9, 18, 22, 27, 34, 45, 48
responsibility 13, 20, 21, 24, 25, 41,
    53–6, 62–6, 71, 98
rewards 74
rights, of parents 54–6, 58, 65, 66, 69,
    78, 88
    of step-parents 137–8
rivalry, sibling 68–9, 143
roles 44–5, 49, 138

role models 12
rows 10, 19, 20, 23, 26, 34, 125, 127–8
    see also conflicts; fighting
rudeness 38, 44–5, 69, 82, 95
rules 23–4, 36, 69–72, 86, 140
    breaking 24, 71–3 passim, 82
    negotiating 69–75
Ryan, Helen 20, 28, 35, 36, 38–40, 46,
    48, 63, 120, 136

safety net 14
sanctions 59, 70, 73, 77–88 passim, 90,
    135
    implementing 84–6, 90
    loopholes 83
school 14, 17, 25, 26, 43, 53, 55, 59–60,
    64, 94, 98–102
    absence/skipping 67, 85, 93, 98,
        100–2, 122, 140
    exclusion 17, 80, 94, 98, 99
    problems at 98–100
self-centredness 23, 119
self-consciousness 11, 124
self-definition 12
self-doubt 119, 130
self-esteem 11, 14, 29, 97, 105, 107,
    119–26, 130
self-hatred 114
self-reliance 13
separation 106, 137
services 25, 79–80
sex 10, 14, 93, 106–8
    information 106–8
    and law 108
sexually transmitted diseases 107
shoplifting 26
shopping 14, 20
shouting 23, 35–6, 43, 56
shyness 124
siblings 43, 138–40, 143
silence 35
smoking 41, 53, 55, 57, 58, 72, 77–9
    passim
Social Services 61, 88, 108
solutions, finding their own 49, 50, 59,
    97
sports 130
starting afresh 87, 90
staying out late 13, 38–9, 53, 70, 86–7
stealing 85, 86, 88, 115
step-parents 23, 24, 34, 137–8, 143 see
    also individual entries

stress 11, 20, 26, 27, 29, 98, 128, 130
successes 64, 76, 120
sulking 25, 81
supervision 28, 62
support 15, 28, 49, 60, 93, 98–9, 101,
    120, 122–3
        between parents 134
swearing 17–19 *passim*, 23, 34, 37–8,
    40, 45, 55, 56, 64, 72, 86

talking 34, 36, 49, 59–60, 66, 97,
    114, 122, 140–1 *see also* abuse;
    communication
talking spoon 76
targets, choosing 72–3, 89
tattoo 94
Taylor, Dawn 44–5, 95, 134
        'Big Roy' 134
        family 38
        Gemma 43, 63–4, 95, 98, 99, 103,
            123, 128, 134, 139–40
        Roy 43, 44, 130, 134, 139–40
telephone 55, 77, 79
tension 26
testing 28, 55, 89, 121
testosterone 10, 11
threats 56, 88, 115
tidying up 25, 41, 58, 62
time management 71, 73
time together 13, 29, 47–8, 80, 120–1,
    124–5, 130
timekeeping 23, 55, 71, 73
tobacco 112
treasure map 123–4
triggers 18, 20–2 *passim*, 30
truancy 98, 100–2
trust 9, 40, 53, 60, 75, 142
TV 79

unity, parents' 134–7, 143

values 23, 45, 70, 97, 121–2, 124, 130
vandalism 26
victim role 18, 42–3, 125
vigilance 28
violence, domestic 24, 26, 34, 88, 142–3
vulnerability 13, 25, 100, 139

Watts, Phil 55, 77, 110
        Sue 12, 19–20, 25, 28, 37, 41, 42,
            48, 55, 57–9 *passim*, 65, 77–9
            passim, 96, 110, 112–13, 126

weight problem 103–4
wind-ups 42–3
withdrawal 34, 36, 37, 45, 128
worry 19, 26, 55